World Heritage Sites of Great Britain and Ireland

Victoria Huxley is an editor and publisher. Geoffrey Smith is a publisher and the author of *100 Best Paintings in London* and co-author (with Deanna MacDonald) of *100 Best Paintings in New York* and *100 Best Paintings in Paris*. They live and work together in Gloucestershire.

United Nations
Educational, Scientific and
Cultural Organization

with the support of the United Kingdom
National Commission for UNESCO

World Heritage Sites
of
Great Britain and Ireland

*An Illustrated Guide to all
27 World Heritage Sites*

Victoria Huxley and Geoffrey Smith

CHASTLETON
An imprint of Arris Publishing Ltd
Gloucestershire

For Lucian, who asked the question

Other books by Geoffrey Smith
100 Best Paintings in London
100 Best Paintings in New York (with Deanna MacDonald)
100 Best Paintings in Paris (with Deanna MacDonald)

First published in Great Britain in 2009 by
CHASTLETON TRAVEL
An imprint of Arris Publishing Ltd
12 Adlestrop, Moreton in Marsh
Gloucestershire GL56 0YN
www.arrisbooks.com

The front cover shows top left: St Kilda Stacs © National Trust for Scotland (photo, Laurie Campbell): top right: The remains of an Engine House near Lavant, Cornwall © Geoffrey Smith; bottom left: Stonehenge, Geoffrey Smith; bottom right: Giant's Causeway © National Trust (photo Chris Hill)

ISBN 978 1 905214 57 0

Printed and bound in Slovenia by Korotan, Ljubljana

Telephone: 01608 659328
Visit our website at www.arrisbooks.com
or email us at info@arrisbooks.com

Every attempt has been made to be accurate on opening times and general visitor
information but it is advisable to double check before planning a visit to any of the sites
as these are subject to change.

CONTENTS

NORTH OF ENGLAND

SCOTLAND

IRELAND

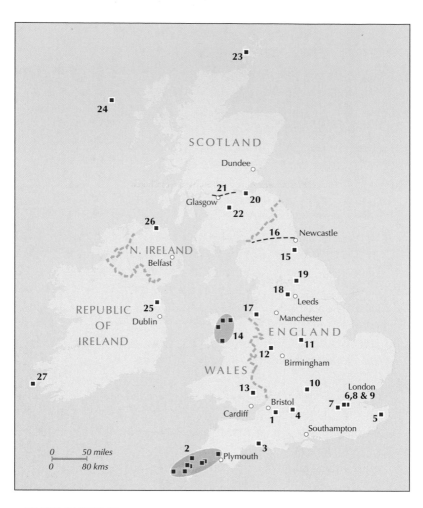

SAMPLE LEGEND

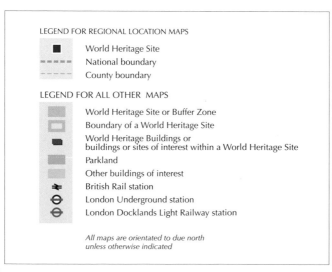

LEGEND FOR REGIONAL LOCATION MAPS

- ■ World Heritage Site
- – – – – – National boundary
- – – – – – County boundary

LEGEND FOR ALL OTHER MAPS

- World Heritage Site or Buffer Zone
- Boundary of a World Heritage Site
- World Heritage Buildings or buildings or sites of interest within a World Heritage Site
- Parkland
- Other buildings of interest
- ⇌ British Rail station
- ⊖ London Underground station
- ⊖ London Docklands Light Railway station

All maps are orientated to due north unless otherwise indicated

SOUTH WEST ENGLAND

1. City of Bath
2. Cornwall and West Devon Mining Landscape
3. Dorset and East Devon Coast (Jurassic Coast)
4. Stonehenge, Avebury and Associated Sites

LONDON AND THE SOUTH EAST

5. Canterbury Cathedral, St Augustine's Abbey and St Martin's Church
6. Maritime Greenwich
7. Royal Botanic Gardens, Kew
8. Tower of London
9. Westminster Palace, Westminster Abbey and St Margaret's Church

CENTRAL

10. Blenheim Palace
11. Derwent Valley Mills
12. Ironbridge Gorge

WALES

13. Blaenavon Industrial Landscape
14. Castles and Towns Walls of Edward I in Gwynedd: Conwy, Beaumaris, Harlech, Caernarfon

NORTH OF ENGLAND

15. Durham Castle and Cathedral
16. Frontiers of the Roman Empire: Hadrian's Wall
17. Liverpool – Maritime Mercantile City
18. Saltaire
19. Studley Royal Park including the ruins of Fountains Abbey

SCOTLAND

20. Old and New Towns of Edinburgh
21. Frontiers of the Roman Empire: The Antonine Wall
22. New Lanark
23. Heart of Neolithic Orkney
24. St Kilda (Hebrides)

IRELAND

25. Archaeological Ensemble of the Bend of the Boyne
26. Giant's Causeway and Causeway Coast
27. Skellig Michael

INTRODUCTION

A couple of years ago one of our sons asked us 'How many World Heritage Sites are there in Britain?' – after stumping up five or six sites including Stonehenge and the Tower of London we tailed off into silence. A conversation ensued which led to plans for this guidebook; we hope it might enthuse others to make a journey to the exciting and beautiful places in Great Britain and Ireland that have been designated by Unesco (The United Nations Educational, Scientific and Cultural Organisation) as World Heritage Sites.

We have tried to show why these sites have been chosen by Unesco. Sometimes, as in the case of Stonehenge it is obvious, other selections have been made on the basis that they are unique, or the first examples of their kind in the world – as is the case for many British industrial heritage sites; others are simply of great natural importance. Writing and researching the book has been a revelatory excursion into Britain's past. We hope that readers will enjoy the same experience.

We have tried to give as much background historical information as is possible in a book of this length as all these sites are much more than simply destinations for a tourist's day out – although they are that too. Overall the 27 current sites present an extraordinary picture of the cultural and economic development of the British Isles from Neolithic times right up to the 20th century. There are also many wild destinations ranging from the remote island archipelago of St Kilda, the circles of Neolithic Orkney to Skellig Michael which is not much more than a lonely rock off the far south-western coast of Ireland.

In our research we have inevitably drawn heavily on the recommendation documents written by Icomos (the International Council on Monuments and Sites) which has a special responsibility as advisor to Unesco on the choice of World Heritage Sites. They debate and establish the criteria regarding which sites are important enough to be considered for this rare status.

History of the World Heritage movement

The idea of protecting heritage dates back to after the end of the First World War, but it was not until 1959 that Unesco was galvanised into action by launching an international campaign to protect the ancient temples of Abu Simbel in Egypt which were about to be flooded as a result of the construction of the Aswan Dam. Other successes followed and in 1972 a Convention concerning the Protection of the World Cultural and Natural Heritage developed to protect both man-made and natural sites. This convention was adopted by the 1972 United Nations Conference on 16 November 1972.

The Unesco website states that 'Heritage is our legacy from the past, what we live with today, and what we pass on to future generations. Our cultural and natural heritage are both irreplaceable sources of life and inspiration. Places as unique and diverse as the wilds of East Africa's Serengeti, the Pyramids of Egypt, the Great Barrier Reef in Australia and the Baroque cathedrals of Latin America make up our world's heritage. What makes the concept of World Heritage exceptional is its universal application. World Heritage sites belong to all the peoples of the world, irrespective of the territory on which they are located.'

It was not until 1986 that seven very varied sites were designated in Great Britain and Ireland. Since then the list has gone from strength to strength and recent research has shown how the designation confers increased awareness of the sites internationally, nationally and locally. They become a badge of honour for the community and their status helps to support them financially, brings lifeblood into the local economy in the shape of visitors and also helps keep unwelcome modern developments at bay.

We would like to thank the following for their help in preparing this book: Sulman Bajwa at the Department of Culture, Media and Sport, Susan Bain, manager of the Western Isles for the National Trust for Scotland, Barbara Birley at the Vindolanda Trust, Susan Black from the National Trust for Northern Ireland for assistance with the Giant's Causeway chapter, Tim and Caroline Bucknall for their hospitality, David Breeze for his help with the chapters on the Antonine Wall and Hadrian's Wall, Roger Clarke, Pamela Reynolds, Dave Shaw and Julie Woodward for their help and encouragement on the chapter on Saltaire, Sean Conlon of Historic Scotland for help with photos of Neolithic Orkney, Stuart Dewar for invaluable assistance on the early Christian saints, Richard Edmonds for his valuable comments on the Jurassic Coast, Rachel Grecian of Northumberland National Park, Anne Heywood at Durham Cathedral, Dr Anthea Jones for her sharp eyes and historical knowledge, Christine Kenyon (CADW) for furnishing photographs for the Welsh castles, Linda Leung at the UK National Commission for UNESCO, Margaret McLeish for help with the photographs of the Antonine Wall, Graham Nisbet of the Hunterian Museum, Glasgow, Tony Roche at the Department of Environment, Heritage and Local Government, Ireland, John Sinclair at the National Trust for Scotland, John Skermer for help with proofreading, Amy Taylor and Torfaen Council for their generous help with Blaenavon, John Taylor for his excellent maps and Su Whiting at Greenwich Council.

Victoria Huxley
Geoffrey Smith

South West England

City of Bath

Cornwall and West Devon Mining Landscape

Dorset and East Devon Coast (Jurassic Coast)

Stonehenge, Avebury and Associated Sites

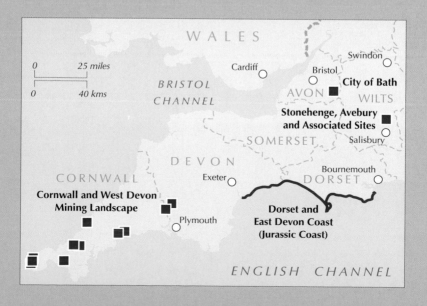

Opposite: An example of one of the many splendid Georgian doorways in the city.

City of Bath

Georgian Elegance and Roman Baths

Date of Inscription 1987

Bath is a city of international significance for its 'contribution to urban design, for its architectural quality, its Roman remains, its Georgian town centre and its historic associations... last but not least, in spite of all the changes imposed upon it by the 20th century, Bath remains a beautiful city, set in a hollow among hills and as architecturally exciting as it was in its Georgian heyday.' (from the inscription of criteria for the city's inclusion as a World Heritage Site.)

Location

Bath is situated near Bristol, in south west Britain, in the county of Somerset.

HISTORY

Bath's long history begins with the legend of Bladud, the father of King Lear. The story goes that after spending 11 years in Athens, Prince Bladud returned home suffering from leprosy. He was banished from court and became a swineherd and, at the village of Swainswick (about three miles from the present city), saw his pigs wallowing in hot water which freed them of scurf and scabs. He followed them into the water and was cured of his leprosy. According to the legend, Bladud became ninth king of the Britons in 863 BC and later founded the city which was called Caer Badon, the city of baths.

When the Romans invaded Britain they rediscovered these sacred springs and constructed their own bath complex as well as a temple. In AD 676 a monastery was built on the site of today's abbey using the stone remains from Roman buildings.

In medieval times Bath became an important centre for the wool trade but it

remained a relatively small walled city until reaching its apogee during the 18th century when the city became a fashionable spa town. Much of it was rebuilt featuring elegant new architecture described by the architectural historian Nikolaus Pevsner as a 'piece of town planning unique in England and indeed in Europe'.

THE ROMAN BATHS

The Romans invaded Britain in AD 43 but it was not for another 20 years, when the situation had become sufficiently peaceful, that the huge bath complex was built with other leisure facilities. They also erected a temple dedicated to the Celtic goddess, Sulis, alongside their own goddess of healing, Minerva.

The engineering skills of the Romans enabled them to build a reservoir to enclose the main spring which could then be controlled to provide water to the bath complex. The Great Bath was lined with lead sheets using lead from the nearby Mendip Hills.

BATH SPRING WATER

- 10,000 years ago rainwater was trapped beneath the Mendips at between 2700–4300 metres depth
- A faultline in the rock strata emerges beneath Bath which allows the heated water to surface
- 1,100,000 litres (240,000 gallons) per day flow from the spring
- 46°C (115° F) is the average temperature
- There are 43 minerals in the water

The baths, open to both men and women, were a centre of social life for the Romans. The spring waters were hot enough to be enjoyed all year round and their curative properties celebrated. Throughout the three centuries of Roman occupation the baths were constantly improved and extended. As well as the tepidarium (the warm room) and the caldarium (hot room), there were cold plunge pools and later a laconium

The magnificent head at the centre of the Temple pediment.

– like a modern-day sauna with a hot dry atmosphere. In the second century a round pool was installed.

Although nothing of the sacred temple can be seen today – its remains are thought to be under Stall Street – one can view the temple pediment with its magnificent central head, a cross between a gorgon and a godlike figure, flanked by winged victories. This masterpiece of both Celtic and Roman significance was found during the building of the Pump Room in 1790. Another 18th-century discovery was the life-size gilded bronze head of the goddess Minerva which must have also graced the temple.

Today one can still, like the Celts and Romans before us, marvel at the sight of the hot spring waters flowing with great force from the depths of the earth. The whole atmosphere is humid and steamy, imbued with a distinct sulphuric smell.

'The fortifications have given way, the buildings raised by giants are crumbling. The roofs have collapsed; the towers are in ruins... There were splendid palaces and many halls with water flowing through them...'

Lines from 'The Ruin', an eighth century poem

The Abbey

At the heart of Bath is the abbey. The buildings on this site have gone through many manifestations before reaching the form we see today. In the seventh century a monastery was built using masonry from the neglected Roman baths; King Edgar of Wessex was crowned here in 963 as the first king of all England. After the Norman invasion, Bath became the seat of the see of Somerset (previously at Wells), the abbey was raised to cathedral status and a programme of rebuilding begun. In the 13th century the Pope returned Wells to cathedral status and instigated an arrangement whereby both cathedrals became dual seats of the bishopric of Bath and Wells. However Wells became the preferred seat of most medieval bishops and Bath Abbey fell into disrepair.

The West Front of the Abbey

In 1499, Oliver King, the bishop of Bath had a dream in which he saw an image of the Holy Trinity with angels ascending and descending a ladder reaching from heaven to earth. Apparently a voice spoke to him, 'Let an Olive establish the Crown and a King restore the Church.' He took this to mean himself and embarked on his mission to raise the abbey to its former glory. The central statue over the west door is of King Henry VII and flanking the door itself are St Peter and St Paul to whom the abbey is dedicated.

In 1499, on a visit to Bath, Oliver King, the bishop, was shocked by the sight of the church in ruins – he is said to have had a dream calling on him to rebuild the abbey. A new cathedral church was completed just a few years before the Dissolution of the Monasteries in 1539 and once more the building was stripped of its lead, iron and glass and left to decay. However, during the reign of Queen Elizabeth I the church was again restored, becoming the grand parish church of the city. In the 19th century another major restoration was carried out by Gilbert Scott and the timber

The west front of Bath Abbey.

roof of the nave was replaced with fan vaulting to match that in the choir, thereby completing Bishop King's original plans.

Today it is one of the most charming churches in England – an abbey only in name – and its rich stained glass and plethora of memorials to the great and good bear testimony to the popularity of Bath and its springs.

Pre-Georgian Bath

The King's Bath was used from Norman times as a place for people to come for a cure but it was in the 16th century that the opportunity of bathing in the 'miraculous' waters became popular. King Charles II visited the city in 1663 and at this time pumps were installed so visitors could drink the waters as well as bathe in them. Queen Mary later claimed that her infertility was cured by bathing in the Cross Bath in 1687. However Bath was seen as an unsophisticated place, still encircled by a medieval stone wall, a destination only for the sick and elderly.

Georgian Bath

Once again a royal visit to Bath in 1702-3 by Queen Anne raised the profile of the city and in her footsteps the Court and its fashionable followers came in considerable numbers. A young gambler called Richard 'Beau' Nash arrived in 1704 and saw the opportunities to be made in the city. In 1705 he was appointed 'Master of Ceremonies' and set about transforming the rigid protocols which then precluded intercourse between the various social strata. In Bath, the middle classes and the aristocracy began to mix under his system of introductions at social functions. He also undertook many improvements for visitors – streets were lit and kept clean, the Assembly Rooms and the Pump Room were built as respectable places for polite

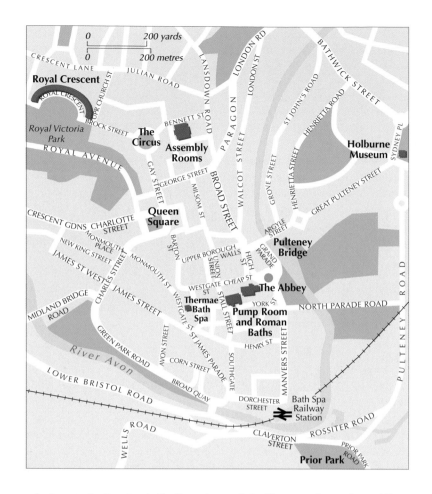

gatherings and glittering balls. Swearing and duelling were banned, gambling – hitherto a reason for much bad behaviour – was put on a more organised basis and Bath became a place where new friendships were forged, marriages made, and seemly entertainments enjoyed.

Beau Nash was a great dandy and leader of fashion. He wore a black wig instead of the customary white, he wore shoes and stockings instead of clumsy boots and for nearly half a century he was known as the 'King of Bath'. As the social milieu improved under his leadership so did the town itself with a rapid increase in bright new buildings made from locally quarried stone. Much of this construction was carried out under the guidance of the architect and builder John Wood. Wood was the son of a humble Bath builder but was nonetheless full of ambition and novel ideas.

The third man whose ideas invigorated

the city was Ralph Allen who made a vast fortune by reforming the local, and then national, postal service. He also acquired the quarries at Bathampton Down and Combe Down which supplied the limestone necessary to rebuild the city. In 1727 he built a Palladian mansion at Prior Park on a hill overlooking Bath – 'To see Bath, and for all Bath to see.' He funded the building of the Mineral Water Hospital and was Bath's MP between 1757-64. He is buried in Claverton churchyard in a pyramid-topped tomb.

The Pump Room

First erected in 1706 in the style of an orangery as a place to drink **Key Sites** the healing waters and gain access to the King's Bath, this was later rebuilt between 1791–95 in a neo-classical style. Today visitors can still enjoy its unique ambience and come to drink the hot spring water, or to have a meal or afternoon tea in elegant and spacious surroundings while listening to the oldest established musical ensemble in Britain, the Pump Room Trio. Above the Tompion clock and sundial is a sculpture of Beau Nash – Ralph Allen's portrait can be seen on the south wall.

Queen Square

This square was the first of John Wood's developments. He brought unity to the north side with its imposing façade in the classical Palladian style. In fact the 'palace front' hides seven town houses. The obelisk in the square gardens was installed by Beau Nash in 1734 with a dedication to the Prince of Orange. The trees are a later addition.

A steep climb up Gay Street from the square lead to the Circus, the Royal Crescent and the Assembly Rooms.

The Circus

This is unquestionably John Wood's masterpiece. Unfortunately he died the year building began in 1754 but his son, John Wood the Younger (1727–81), completed the project. John Wood was hugely interested in the Druids and the diameter

A section of the Circus seen through the branches of the central plane trees.

Detail of the mouldings in the Circus, probably based on Masonic symbols.

of the Circus is based on Wood's measurements of Stonehenge. The stone acorns which decorate its parapet recall the legend of how Bladud found the hot springs. It is possible that John Wood also intended the circus to be a representation of a temple to the Sun allied to the crescent moon of the Royal Crescent.

The Circus was originally called the King's Circus and was entirely paved; the centrepiece of magnificent plane trees were introduced early in the 19th century. Each house bears three rows of columns, Tuscan, Ionic and Corinthian. Masonic symbols are believed to be the inspiration for the carvings above the first row of pillars. The houses are of different sizes because of the curved sections and inside the rooms are graceful and high-ceilinged.

THE ROYAL CRESCENT

The younger Wood continued his father's ambitious innovations in 1767–74 with the construction of the first crescent-shaped architectural ensemble in Britain. Unlike the closed effect of the Circus, the Crescent looks out to the green hills which enclose the city. There are 30 opulent houses with 114 Ionic columns but no further decoration interrupts the gracious sweep of fine stone. No. 1 Royal Crescent has been preserved as a museum and is open to visitors.

To finance their building programme the Woods leased land for speculative building from the freeholder and sub-leased to other builders for work behind the frontages. Those builders in turn would be financed by tenancy agreements for long leases and

One of the central houses in the Royal Crescent.

could borrow with these as security. Since Bath was overflowing with visitors demand always outstripped supply and so these arrangements proved to be sound investments.

THE ASSEMBLY ROOMS

Just east of the Circus, the present building was designed by John Wood the Younger in 1769–71. The large ballroom could accommodate over a thousand people for dances. Now the building houses the excellent Museum of Costume showing fashions from the last 400 years. It still retains its original and exquisite chandeliers.

PULTENEY BRIDGE

Designed by Robert Adam and built in 1770 for the landowner William Pulteney, the bridge (see picture below) was constructed to gain access to Bathwick across the River Avon. Pulteney wanted to build a complete suburb at Bathwick but his money ran out and only the bridge itself, Great Pulteney Street, the Sydney Hotel and Pleasure Gardens were completed. The bridge is supported by three beautifully proportioned arches and is lined with shops on both sides.

HOLBURNE MUSEUM

At the end of the wide and imposing Great Pulteney Street the museum was built in 1795 as a set of public rooms alongside the Pleasure Gardens. It now holds regular exhibitions of fine art.

PRIOR PARK

Ralph Allen's mansion was built between 1735 and 1750. The architect was John Wood the elder although he quarrelled with Allen and the work was completed by Richard Jones, Allen's clerk of works. Nikolaus Pevsner describes it as 'the most ambitious and the most complete re-creation of Palladio's villas on English soil'. The landscaped garden is now owned by the National Trust and has marvellous panoramic views of the city. The poet, Alexander Pope, and later, the great landscape gardener, Capability Brown, designed the gardens, constructing several lakes, a Gothick temple, a grotto named after Mrs Allen and a very beautiful Palladian bridge which spans the serpentine lake.

The large and impressive house, now owned by Prior Park College, is 15 bays wide with a huge central portico of six columns.

THE MODERN THERMAL SPA

The Thermae Bath Spa complex in Hot Bath Street offers a centre for modern bathing in Bath's natural springs. There is an open air rooftop pool with views of the city plus four glass steam rooms, treatment and massage rooms.

VISITOR INFORMATION

HOW TO GET THERE

There are regular train services from London Paddington and Waterloo. National Rail Enquiries: 08457 484950 From abroad: 44 (0) 20 7278 5240 www.nationalrail.co.uk

National Express have regular coach travel linking all major towns and cities in UK. Information: www.gobycoach.co.uk

Bristol International Airport is 15 miles from Bath; www.bristolairport.co.uk

Bath is just 10 miles from junction 18 of the M4 motorway and there are three Park & Ride car parks around the city. Information: www.bathnes.gov.uk

OPENING TIMES

ASSEMBLY ROOMS 01225 477789
March to October 11.00 am – 6.00 pm
November to February 11.00 am – 5.00 pm

ROMAN BATHS AND PUMP ROOM 01225 477743
January to February & November to December 9.30 am - Last admission 4.30 pm
Closed 25 and 26 December
March to June & September to October 9.00 am; Last admission 5.00 pm
July to August 9.00 am; Last admission 9.00 pm

HOLBURNE MUSEUM 01225 466669
Tuesday – Saturday 10.00 am – 5.00 pm Sunday 11.00 am – 5.00 pm
Closed Mondays except Bank Holidays 11.00 am – 5.00 pm

PRIOR PARK 01225 833422
March – October 11.00 am – 5.30 pm every day except Tuesday
November – January 11.00 am – Dusk – Saturday and Sunday only

NO 1 ROYAL CRESCENT 01225 428126
Tuesday to Sunday and Bank Holiday Mondays 10.30 am – 5.00 pm (4 pm in November only). Closed Good Friday

WHERE TO STAY

There is a plethora of good hotels and bed and guest houses in the city. The best place to start is with the Bath Tourist Information Centre in Abbey Church Yard who, for a nominal fee, can book accommodation for you. Email: tourism@bathtourism.co.uk Tel: 0870 420 1278 Fax: 01225 47787 Tel: +44 (0)870 444 6442 (overseas visitors only)

www.visitbath.co.uk

The Royal Crescent Hotel 01225 823333 www.royalcrescent.co.uk

Dukes Hotel 01225 787960 www.dukesbath.co.uk

Mrs Johnson's B & B 47 Sydney Buildings 01225 463033 www.sydneybuildings.co.uk

Opposite: The remains of a Cornish engine house near Lavant.

Cornwall and West Devon Mining Landscape

Pioneering Engineers and Mining Communities

Date of Inscription 2006

Why is this a World Heritage Site?

Cornwall is famous for its wild and beautiful coastline and its picturesque coastal villages – but as visitors scan this unique landscape they will notice chimneys dotted here and there, strangely shaped grassland and open quarries – these record the remains of Cornwall's industrial past much of which has now gained World Heritage status.

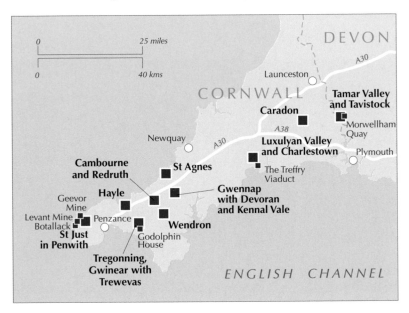

History

The development of the mines in Cornwall was crucial to the world's first Industrial Revolution because many of the innovations that facilitated mining in the area, such as the steam engine, were vital to industrialisation in Britain and would later help to drive the machines of the world. The growth of deep underground mines, their engine houses – or 'Wheals' – the foundries, the new harbours such as Charlestown, the expansion of ports, new housing for ancillary workers and grand houses and beautiful gardens for the mine owners, all transformed the county.

In the mining slump of the 1860s, numerous Cornish miners emigrated and exported their expertise to Australia, South Africa and Central and South America. As the saying goes, 'If you look down a hole, you'll find a Cornishman at the bottom of it.'

The sites are many and various and comprise some of the most authentic surviving components of the mining industry in Cornwall and West Devon from around 1700 to 1914.

St Just in Penwith

On the north coast, along the B3306 lie many of the most impressive mining sites along a rugged coastline. Much of St Just was built to serve the local mining community. There is a pub called the Miner's Arms and the impressive Portledden House was the home of a mine owner.

Key Sites

Levant mine

This dramatically sited mine has the oldest beam engine in Cornwall, the only engine at a tin or copper mine still powered by steam. The mine closed in 1930 but it has been restored and visitors can now go underground and view the winding and pumping shafts. Its workings run under the sea for over a mile.

Botallack

The Botallack Count House, a short walk from the Lavant mine, now restored by the National Trust, was the mining company's account house where miners received their pay. The remains of the precariously sited mine are situated on a promontory above the sea. In 1846 it was visited by Queen Victoria and Prince Albert.

Geevor mine

This was the last working tin mine in Cornwall, finally abandoned in 1990. The site is now the Geevor Tin Mine Museum with mining exhibits and excellent guided tours around the huge drying and washing sheds where everything is coated in red dust from the minerals. Visitors can also go into the Wheal Mexico mine for an authentic experience of 18th-century workings.

Godolphin House

This splendid granite house (see picture below) was built by the Godolphin family on the proceeds of the family's successful tin mining. Sir William Godophin was five times sheriff of the county and comptroller of the coinage of tin (a tax on refined tin payable to the Crown). His son was appointed Master of the Mines by Henry VIII. The Godolphins were also great innovators and at Wheal Vor

THE PIONEERS AND THEIR INVENTIONS

THOMAS NEWCOMEN 1663–1729

Thomas Newcomen was an ironmonger who was born in Dartmouth, Devon. Newcomen perfected the atmospheric steam engine used to pump water out of deep mines. Thomas Savery's pump of 1698 had used condensed steam to make a vacuum which sucked water from the bottom of the mine shaft but was limited to a depth of only thirty feet. Newcomen replaced Savery's condensing vessel with a cylinder containing a piston; the vacuum was now used to move the piston which was attached to a beam – the beam in turn was attach by a chain to a pump at the bottom of the mine. His engines were reliable but expensive. Nevertheless they were used by Cornish mine owners and there were approximately 100 engines in use in Britain and Europe when Newcomen died in 1729.

RICHARD TREVITHICK 1771–1833

Strong and tall, Trevithick was known as the 'Cornish Giant'. He started work with his father at Wheal Treasury mine where he soon displayed precocious engineering skills. He later became engineer at the Ding Dong mine in Penzance where in the late 1790s he developed a high-pressure steam engine for raising ore and refuse from the mines. In 1801 he had progressed to a larger steam road locomotive known as the Puffing Devil; this was followed by the Penydarren locomotive in 1804 which was the world's first steam engine to run successfully – 26 years before George Stephenson's Rocket. However, his business acumen did not match his engineering genius; he failed to get financial support for his ideas and left Britain in 1816 to work in Peru. He returned penniless to Cornwall and died in 1833 at the age of 62.

WILLIAM BICKFORD 1774–1834

Although William Bickford was not involved in the mining industry himself – he was a currier and a leather merchant – he was concerned about the accidents caused by the use of gunpowder in the tin mines. He invented the safety fuse which is still in use today practically unchanged. Its use has saved hundreds of lives. Prior to its invention, gunpowder was inserted in goose quills or rushes to attempt to slow down the flame but accidents were common. Bickford's inspiration for his invention came whilst watching ropes being made. He realised that if a strand of yarn impregnated with gunpowder was incorporated into a rope (which was then surrounded with tarred twine to add strength and waterproofing), the result would be a reliable and predictable fuse. The 'safety rods' as he called them were first made commercially in 1831 at a factory at Tuckingmill between Redruth and Camborne.

SIR HUMPHRY DAVY 1778–1829

Humphry Davy was born in Penzance (where there is a statue to him). His achievements were many: he discovered the anaesthetic effects of laughing gas (nitrous oxide) and his researches led to the isolation and naming of seven previously unknown elements. In 1815 he was asked to help in the control of mine explosions. His response was the safety lamp. Before this miners, who had to rely on naked flames in order to see, were in constant danger from flammable methane concentrations in deep mines. Davy realised that if he enclosed the flame with a piece of metal gauze, the heat would be distributed over the area of the gauze but would not reach ignition temperature (for the methane) at any one point.

developed the use of gunpowder below the ground in the late 17th century (known as 'shooting the rocks'). They also installed a 'blowing house' invented by Richard Carew which was used to reduce the ore to powder. In 1716 they installed one of Thomas Newcomen's atmospheric steam engines.

CAMBORNE AND REDRUTH

The granite ridge that dominates the area produced some of the richest and deepest copper and tin mines in the world which resulted in the expansion of these towns along with many new public amenities such as the School of Science and Art in Redruth. Both towns maintain their 19th-century lay-out.

ST AGNES

The landscape of St Agnes has been shaped by mining. Many engine houses still remain including Wheal Coates mine, now a dramatic ruin with three engine houses for winding, pumping and stamping. The miners' cottages with their surrounding fields where crops were grown for their families can still be seen.

THE TREFFRY VIADUCT

This unique viaduct was built between 1839-42 by Joseph Treffry who owned the Fowey Consuls mine and built Par Harbour where up to 50 ships could be accommodated. Tucked away in the exquisite and unspoilt Luxulyan Valley it consists of ten arches and is nearly 30 metres (100 ft) high – 200,000 cubic ft of granite was used in its construction. Granite was taken by horse-drawn carriages along the viaduct and joined the railway. At the same time a lower tier served as an aqueduct which turned 13 water wheels in the valley. It is possible to walk across the top of the viaduct and explore the network of canals.

CHARLESTOWN

A small port on the south coast (A390), a real gem, now used extensively by the film industry. The harbour was designed by John Smeaton at the end of the 18th century. It was built by a local industrialist to export copper ore and china clay.

The picturesque setting of Charlestown harbour built in the 18th century to handle industrial exports.

GWENNAP WITH DEVORAN AND KENNAL VALE

To the south east of Redruth, between the A393 and the A39 are extensive remains of copper mines, shafts and the railways that ran between the mines and the ports. Gwennap was once described as the 'richest square mile in the Old World'. It is here especially that the landscape shows the scars of copper mining. Copper was worked from at least 1718 at Wheal Busy. The best mines of the district were those south of St Day and over a quarter of the Gwennap parish worked in the United Mine which ranged over a mile and half under the green fields.

GWENNAP PIT

The great founder of Methodism, John Wesley, liked to preach here. This hollow is thought to have been caused by the surface collapsing into an abandoned mine below. It does not collect water which adds credence to this theory. Its first use for preaching was on 6 September 1762. John Wesley wrote, 'The wind was so high that I could not stand at the usual place at Gwennap; but at a small distance was a hollow capable of containing many thousands of people. I stood on one side of this amphitheatre towards the top and with people beneath on all sides.'

The Pit is still used for religious gatherings to this day. The circular terraces were cut by local miners between 1803 and 1806.

TAMAR VALLEY AND TAVISTOCK

The biggest mine in the nominated area – the Devon Great Consols was situated in West Devon – once the richest copper mine in Europe, its arsenic output also dominated the world's supply. Although very toxic, arsenic has many medicinal and industrial uses. The nearest town on the Tamar is Tavistock which underwent extensive changes in the 19th century under the guiding hand of the landowner, Francis Russell, the 7th Duke of Bedford, and his steward John Benson. They utilised the profits from the mine to clear slums and put up many fine public buildings which can still be seen today such as the Guildhall (1863), Town Hall (1860), Cornmarket

Statue of the Duke of Bedford in Tavistock town centre. He was a major landowner in the area.

(1835) and Fitzford Church. Many are built of the green volcanic Hurdwick Stone quarried locally and granite from the Pew Tor on Dartmoor. The duke built model homes for the mineworkers and their families – the cottages were built at an average cost of £22 each – and also funded schooling for their children.

Tavistock was linked to the port of Morwellham by the Tavistock Canal built between 1803-17. Over 4 miles (about 7 km) long it is still well maintained and includes a tunnel about one mile long (1.6 km).

Brief History of Mining in Cornwall and Devon

Bronze Age	Tin trade between Cornwall and the Mediterranean
1296	Cornish miners sent to royal silver mines at Combe Martin, Devon
Mid-15th century	Underground tin mines develop especially in Gwennap and St Just
1547	Tin production peaks
1600s	Cornish mining engineers advise the government and the Mines Royal throughout British Isles
1690s	The use of gunpowder revolutionises hard-rock mining
1712	Thomas Newcomen and John Calley build first atmospheric steam engine to pump water out of a mine
1714	John Coster patents water-powered pumping engine
1720-70	Cornwall becomes the world's largest producer of copper
1802	Richard Trevithick is granted the first patent for a working high-pressure steam engine
1831	William Bickford invents the safety fuse
1860s	Cornish mining peaks in copper. By-products such as arsenic, lead and silver also produced
1870s	Copper industry collapses and tin becomes the pre-eminent mineral
20th century	Most mines close as the price of tin drops.

Morwellham Quay, showing the railway used to transport mined materials to the waiting ships.

The mines were all placed around the River Tamar and small quays were built to ship out the mined material mainly to Calstock in Cornwall; the East Cornwall Mineral Railway also built a link between the mines and the port.

MORWELLHAM QUAY

Morwellham Quay is 4 miles (about 7 km) from Tavistock and is now a museum and visitor centre. Copper ore was taken from the nearby George and Charlotte mines (believed to be named after George III and his consort). It is thought the mine began in the mid-18th century alongside the William and Mary mine which is known to have been in operation in 1718. Today many of the buildings used to house the mine can still be seen as well as water wheels, winches, tramways and lime kilns. The assayer's laboratory and his house can be visited next to the Smithy. Behind the quay across the large green is a row of large, well-made houses built by the Duke of Bedford for his workers which are still in use today.

A MINER'S LIFE

Miners were badly paid and their working lives were hazardous in the extreme. There was constant danger from a possible collapse of timbers supporting the tunnel ceiling, from falling rocks and from accidental explosions of blasting powder before the advent of the safety fuse. In deep workings where underground temperatures could reach over 100°F (38°C), miners' lungs were damaged by fumes. They worked for 8-10 hours in these terrible conditions lit only by the weak light of candles and at the end of the day they were often faced with long climbs back to the surface up slippery wooden ladders in the dark. As the graveyards attest, many men and boys slipped to their deaths when they were too exhausted to hold on to the ladders.

In addition many deep workings were susceptible to sudden flooding as in the 1880s when heavy rainfall on Dartmoor caused the River Tavy to rise, flooding the East Crowndale mine near Morwellham Quay, resulting in the drowning of three miners.

See www.visitcornwall.co.uk 01872 322900
email:tourism@cornwallenterprise.co.uk

24 towns in Cornwall have their own tourist information centres to offer advice on accommodation and other attractions.

For Tamar Valley and Tavistock contact the Tourist Information Centre 01822 612938

How to get there

For local public transport information 0870 608 2608 www.travelinesw.com

Rail travel between Penzance and other cities including London Paddington is fast and frequent. There are mainline railway stations at Bodmin, Redruth, St Austell, Truro, Newquay, St Ives and Falmouth.

For Tavistock take the same line from Paddington and alight at Plymouth. A regular bus service runs between Plymouth, Tavistock and other local towns.

National Rail Enquiries: 08457 484950 From abroad: 44 (0) 20 7278 5240 www.nationalrail.co.uk

Opening times

Levant Mine

01736 786156 www.nationaltrust.org.uk

Botallack Mine and Count House Workshop

01736 788588 www.nationaltrust.org.uk

For both of the above (check with website)
Steaming
7 – 28 March Fridays 11.00 am – 5.00 pm
2 April – 30 May Wednesday and Fridays 11.00 am – 5.00 pm
June Wednesday – Friday and Sundays 11.00 am – 5.00 pm
1 July – 30 September Tuesday – Friday and Sunday 11.00 am – 5.00 pm
October Wednesday and Friday 11.00 am – 5.00 pm
Not Steaming
February Friday 11.00 am – 4.00 pm
7 November – 30 January 11.00 am – 4.00 pm
Open Bank Holiday Sundays and Mondays

Geevor Mine

01736 788662   www.geevor.com

Open every day except Saturday all year round
Easter – October 9.00 am – 5.00 pm (tours on the hour from 10.00 am until 4.00 pm)
November – Easter 9.00 am – 4pm (tours at 11.00 am, 1.00 and 3.00 pm)
During school holidays underground tours run continuously

Godolphin House

:01736 763194 www.godolphinhouse.com

Easter – 2 November garden open daily 10.00 am – 5.00 pm
14 May – 29 October house open Wednesdays 11.00 am – 5.00 pm. Also open many other days in summer, ring to check.

Morwellham Quay

01822 833808 www.morwhellham-quay.co.uk

Open every day except Christmas Day, Boxing Day and New Year's Day
October – February 10.00 am – 4.30 pm (last entry 2.30 pm)
March – October 10.00 am – 5.30 pm (last entry 3.30 pm)

Where to Stay

For Redruth, Camborne and Hayle
Crossroads Lodge 01209 820551 www.hotelstruro.com
For St Agnes
Penkerris 01872 552262 www.penkerris.co.uk
For Truro
Tourist Information Centre 01872 274555
Royal Hotel 01872 270345 www.royalhotelcornwall.co.uk
For St Just in Penwith
Tourist Information Centre 01736 788669
The Star Inn 01736 788767
For Charlestown
T'Gallants 01726 70203
For Tamar Valley and Tavistock
Browns 01822 618686 www.brownsdevon.co.uk
The Horn of Plenty 01822 832528 www.thehornofplenty.co.uk
April Cottage 01822 613280

*Opposite: Folded bands of Upper Jurassic limestone march across
the beach towards Osmington, east of Weymouth.*

Dorset and East Devon Coast (Jurassic Coast)

A Living Museum of Geology

Date of Inscription 2001

Why is this a World Heritage Site?

A beautiful and dramatic stretch of Britain's coastline, the Jurassic Coast is a geological time capsule displaying approximately 185 million years of the Earth's history. In almost continuous sequence erosion has revealed rock formations from the Triassic, Jurassic and Cretaceous periods spanning the Mesozoic Era. The site also contains a range of internationally important fossil deposits that have produced well-preserved and diverse evidence of Mesozoic life.

Location

The area known as the Jurassic Coast runs for 95 miles (155 km) from Exmouth in East Devon through West Dorset, Weymouth and Portland to Old Harry Rocks in Purbeck. The designated area takes up a narrow coastal strip of land lying between the top of the cliffs and the low water mark.

EXMOUTH TO SIDMOUTH

Orcombe Point, east of Exmouth, marks the western extremity of the Jurassic Coast World Heritage Site featuring rock formations which date back to the beginning of the Triassic period 250 million years ago. Prince Charles opened the Geoneedle Monument on the cliff top in 2002 to mark the inauguration of the site.

East Devon was a desert during the Triassic period some 250–200 million years ago. It was part of the Pangaea landmass which later divided to form our modern continents. The World Heritage Site lies within the dry heart of Pangaea and the desert conditions led to the formation of red rocks that now form the cliffs. Red predominates because deserts have few living organisms and without organic matter iron deposits form red oxides in the rock. Today the Namib desert in East Africa mimics the conditions once found in East Devon.

One of the best way to view this coast is on a boat excursion from Exmouth.

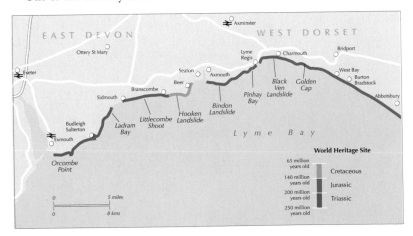

These stacks at Ladrum Bay have been formed by erosion over thousands of years.

Access to the beaches can be found at Exmouth, Sandy Bay, Budleigh Salterton, Ladram, Sidmouth, Branscombe, Beer and Seaton. At Ladram Bay the red rocks have been eroded into spectacular sea stacks.

At Budleigh Salterton the beach is made up of pebbles from an ancient river that once flowed across the desert. As the rocks erode the pebbles are released onto the beach. They are very hard quartzite and unlike any other type found in southern England although they are identical to some 440 million-year-old formations in northern France.

Sidmouth to Seaton

Travelling east from Sidmouth the Triassic rocks are overlaid by rocks from the later Cretaceous period. This creates wonderful scenery where the vibrant red rocks are topped by yellow Upper Greensand rock and white chalk.

At the fishing village of Beer, once famous for its smuggling activities, the bay

The red cliffs looking east from Sidmouth were formed over 200 million years ago.

is surrounded by white chalk cliffs which were formed in shallow sub-tropical seas during the Cretaceous period about 90 million years ago. The Beer Quarry Caves just behind the village were excavated for Beer Stone, a layer within the chalk composed of tiny shell fragments which make a dense rock used for masonry. The earliest workings date from Roman times.

AXMOUTH TO LYME REGIS AND THE UNDERCLIFF

This part of the site is a National Nature Reserve and is a wild and untamed area. The whole reserve is made up of landslides – which are still happening – creating a unique variety of habitats with their own flora and fauna. All visitors must keep to the South West Coast Path that runs through it. You can gain access to the beach at Axmouth and Lyme Regis or take a boat trip from Lyme to see the coast from there.

> ## THE BINDON LANDSLIDE
>
> In 1839 an enormous piece of land, named Goat Island by the locals, tumbled towards the sea and left a deep gorge. Thousands of people visited it and contemporary engravings show how the landscape has changed today partly obscuring the chasm with dense growth of woodlands and shrubs.

The beaches between Lyme and Charmouth (see below) are famous for fossils. Mary Anning (1799–1847), who lived in Lyme, discovered the first ichthyosaur, plesiosaurs (marine reptiles) and flying reptiles to come to the attention of scientists despite having no formal education. Her knowledge of anatomy and her discoveries led her to be described as 'the greatest fossilist who ever lived'.

Her careful documentation of her finds was studied by geologists and helped Charles Darwin formulate his theory on evolution.

Important fossil finds continue to be made by local collectors, especially during the winter when storms batter the cliffs and mudslides are more likely to occur. The beaches are littered with common fossils such as ammonites and belemnites that anyone can search for as the tide goes out although it is dangerous to go too near the cliffs because of rock falls and mudflows; the beach is the safest and most productive place to search especially after a period of rough weather.

Charmouth Beach – famous for its fossils.

LYME REGIS TO BURTON BRADSTOCK

This stretch of the coast is memorable for its high cliffs, dangerous mud and land slides. Beach access is possible at Lyme, Charmouth, Seatown, Eype, West Bay, Freshwater and Burton Bradstock. Charmouth beach, as mentioned above, is an excellent place to search for fossils at low tide.

The towering sandstone cliffs of West Bay and Burton Bradstock are about 180 million years old. The striking layers are like pages in a book with the oldest at the bottom and younger layers above.

The South West Coastal Path has marvellous views of the coastline, much of which is managed and owned by the National Trust. Black Ven between Lyme Regis and Charmouth was the site of one of the largest mudslides in Europe in 1958–9 and is a reminder of how dangerous this coastline can be and how it is still in a state of geological flux.

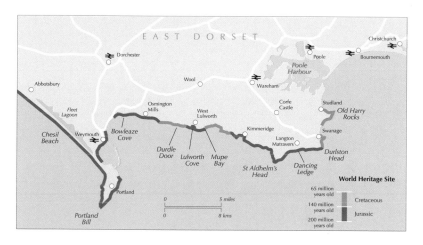

CHESIL BEACH

At 17 miles (28 km) long, Chesil Beach is one of the most impressive barrier beaches in the world, protecting the Fleet Lagoon behind. The beach is a most interesting place to visit simply to look at its pebbles. At West Bay these are like small peas but further east they increase in mass until at Portland, they are the size of large potatoes. This may be caused by the action of the waves which move the larger pebbles faster laterally. It is said that in the days before electronic navigational aids local fishermen landing on the beach at night or in fog could tell exactly where they were from the size of the pebbles.

You can gain access to Chesil Beach via West Bay, Burton Bradstock, Cogden Beach, West Bexington, Abbotsbury, Ferrybridge and Chesil Cove on Portland.

THE FLEET LAGOON

The lagoon is a wildlife reserve rich in fresh and salt water species. It is home to many water birds as well as huge numbers of swans at Abbotsbury. Underneath the water, meadows of eelgrass move in the strong currents and at the mouth of the lagoon there are varieties of seaweed, anemones and sponges.

'The Spirit of Portland' Chesil Beach is one of the finest barrier beaches in the world, linking the Isle of Portland to the mainland. Portland is the source of Portland Stone, one of the highest quality building stones in the world.

THE ISLE OF PORTLAND

Famous for its superb white limestone, this island has been quarried for millennia. The stone was chosen by Christopher Wren for the rebuilding of St Paul's Cathedral in the mid-17th century. Quarrying has created a unique landscape of rock outcrops and drystone walls that can be explored through a network of tracks and trails. This landscape is rich in geology and wildlife.

Tout Quarry features many intriguing works of sculpture. In the spring and early summer unusual plants grow on the thin layer of limestone, and insects, especially butterflies, abound here. Dinosaur footprints were recently uncovered in a working quarry on the island.

Places of interest include the Portland Bill Visitor Centre, Portland Museum, Portland Castle, the disused quarries in the north of the Island and the Coast Path that runs right around it.

WEYMOUTH TO LULWORTH

This area is also known as the Isle of Purbeck. Eastwards from Weymouth the interesting features of this coastline multiply. The cliffs are created from Upper Jurassic and Cretaceous clays, limestones and sandstones and the rocks have been tilted to steep angles by unimaginable forces deep within the Earth.

The coast near to Osmington Mills is a perfect location to see the fossilised burrows and markings made by ancient marine animals.

Lulworth Cove is a beautiful bay forming a perfect horseshoe shape where the soft and hard rocks have been eroded at different rates by the sea. At Stair Hole you can find a viewing platform to see what is called the 'Lulworth Crumple' – a pattern of striated and folded rock created by huge earth movements that happened during the same time that the Alps were formed.

Durdle Door is half a mile west of Lulworth – a sublime arch of hard limestone.

Stair Hole and Lulworth Cove are among the best places to see how the 'grain' of the geology and the hard and soft layers are weathered into bays and headlands. Lulworth, in the distance, is a perfect cove while Stair Hole in the foreground marks the start of the process.

Beach access can be found at Bowleaze Cove, Osmington, Ringstead, Durdle Door and Lulworth Cove and visitors can join boat trips from Weymouth and Lulworth. The famous Fossil Forest is located just east of Lulworth Cove and can be accessed by walking along the beach and over the cliffs (distance one mile). The forest lies within the Army Artillery Ranges that are typically open to the public during school holidays and most, but not all, weekends.

At Flowers Barrow you can see the remains of an Iron Age hill fort built about 2,500 years ago. This impressive site vividly shows the effect of coastal erosion as at least half of the hill fort is now missing – having fallen into the sea.

THE FOSSIL FOREST

For a brief moment in geological time about 144 million years ago sea levels dropped and islands were formed. Soils were created and a forest flourished only to be drowned under a lagoon. Thick mats of algae grew across the forest floor and around the trees. Today this algal growth can be seen as doughnut-shaped structures with a hole in the middle where trees once stood. Fallen logs can also be observed.

KIMMERIDGE, DURLSTON AND SWANAGE

A green headland at Kimmeridge Bay has an oilfield on its cliff top but this has not spoilt the rocky beach where ledges of limestone reach into the sea making it an ideal place for observing marine wildlife.

The Isle of Purbeck is famous for the Purbeck Beds, a complex sequence of limestones and clays that are famous for fossils, both large and small, including dinosaur footprints and minute mammal remains. The character of Swanage and the surrounding villages is entirely due to the use of local stone quarried from the landscape but its stone flags also pave the streets of London while Purbeck Marble (not really marble but a limestone which can be polished) can be found in virtually every church and cathedral in southern England.

OIL UNDER THE SEA

At Bran Point near Osmington faint traces of oil can sometimes be observed on the sea during calm weather. This provided geologists with evidence that oil might be trapped deep in the rock strata and helped lead to discoveries at Kimmeridge and under Poole Harbour.

Durlston Head and its country park offer fine viewpoints of the Isle of Wight, Durlston Bay and the English Channel. Steep limestone cliffs rise up to the east from St Aldhelm's Head and form a haven for nesting sea birds such as kittiwakes and puffins.

The Durlston Visitor Centre will give information on wildlife – both aquatic and airborne – daily. In season there is a live video link of the seabird colony with a soundtrack of birdsong.

OLD HARRY

The World Heritage Site ends at Studland Bay. The headland of Ballard Down is formed from white chalk cliffs that have been eroded into caves, arches and sea stacks including Old Harry Rocks. There are boats trips from Poole Harbour and Swanage which allow you to see these formations clearly.

The chalk downland above the cliffs is owned by the National Trust and supports many species of butterflies and flowers attracted by the clear air and soil.

Old Harry Rocks, the most easterly part of the site and the youngest rock layers.

Visitor Information

For information on the Jurassic Coast please visit this excellent website: www.jurassiccoast.com

How to get there

By road

The M5 provides the main route from most parts of England to the western section of the Jurassic Coast, taking the visitor to within a few miles of Exmouth. From Exmouth the B3178 takes you to Budleigh Salterton and one can take the A3052 for Sidmouth, Seaton and Lyme Regis.

From London take the M3 and the M27 west, then the A31: for Swanage, skirt Bournemouth and take the A351; for Lulworth leave the A351 at Wareham taking the A352 and B3070; for Weymouth and Portland continue on the A31, then the A35 and then take the A354 south from Dorchester.

By bus

The Jurassic Coast Bus Service connects Exeter, Sidford, Beer, Seaton, Lyme Regis, Charmouth, Bridport, Abbotsbury, Weymouth, Wool, Wareham and Poole (Summer service). The buses run every two hours, including a Sunday service. Tickets are £6 for unlimited travel for a day.

By rail

Exeter, Weymouth and Bournemouth have good rail links with London and connections to other parts of England.

Where to stay

Exmouth

Tourist Information Centre 01395 222299
The Barn Hotel 01395 224411 www.barnhotel.co.uk

Budleigh Salterton

Tourist Information Centre 01395 445275
Hansard House Hotel 01395 442773 www.hansardhousehotel.co.uk
Downderry House B & B 01395 442663 www.downderryhouse.co.uk

Sidmouth

Tourist Information Centre 01395 516441
The Royal Glen Hotel 01395 513221 www.royalglenhotel.co.uk

Lyme Regis

Tourist Information Centre 01297 442138
The Royal Lion Hotel 01297 445622 www.royallionhotel.com
The White House B & B 01297 443420 www.lymeregis.com/thewhitehouse

Weymouth

Tourist Information Centre 01305 785747
Windsor Hotel 01305 786540 www.hotel-windsor.co.uk
Wilton Guest House 01305 782820 www.thewiltonhouse.co.uk

Swanage

Tourist Information Centre 01929 422885
Jasper Knights Guest House 01929 424453 www.thejaspers.co.uk

Corfe Castle

Bankes Arms Hotel 01929 480206 www.dorset-hotel.co.uk

Opposite: The sarsen stone megaliths of Stonehenge.

Stonehenge, Avebury and Associated Sites

Ancient and Mysterious Remains

Date of Inscription 1986

Why are they World Heritage Sites?

Stonehenge and Avebury are among the most famous groups of megaliths in the world. The two sanctuaries consist of circles of menhirs arranged in a pattern whose astronomical significance is still being explored. These holy places and the nearby sites are an incomparable testimony to prehistoric rituals from the Neolithic period to the Bronze Age.

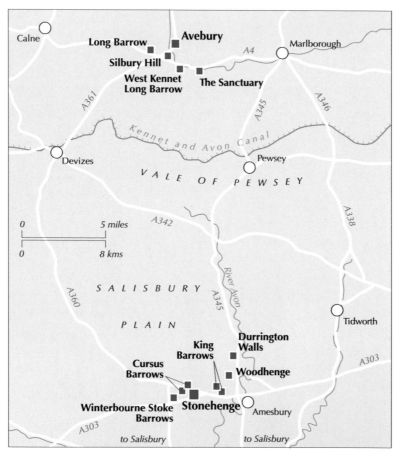

Stonehenge has been regarded as one of the wonders of the world since the 12th century when its existence was recorded by the chroniclers Henry of Huntington and Geoffrey of Monmouth. In the 17th century Stonehenge was the focus of a study by the great architect Inigo Jones. Today one can only walk around Stonehenge, the stones of which are set high among the rolling uplands of Salisbury Plain. The circle has a powerful quietude and grandeur that dwarfs the clutter of modern roads and the traffic that passes nearby.

Both ancient monuments are situated on Salisbury Plain in Wiltshire. Many ancient tracks that were used by prehistoric man meet on the plain and this may be why these great constructions were placed there. From Cornwall, the south coast, Kent, East Anglia, the Midlands, the north of England and Wales many upland ridges rising above the surrounding woodland, cross the country to converge on the plain. The Harroway, for example, ran from Dover along chalk ridges to Stonehenge.

Location

Several stages of construction have been identified:

Stonehenge

1. The first henge was built about 5,000 years ago, around 3,100 BC and was a circle of timbers surrounded by a ditch and bank. These early builders used antlers as pickaxes to break the soil and then shoulder-blade bones of oxen to shovel away the loose earth. Within the bank there are 56 holes named after the 17th-century antiquarian, John Aubrey, who first noticed them. It is known that these holes were for timber posts. Chalk balls, flint rods and cups were found buried in the Aubrey holes which the archaeologist Dr Aubrey Burl believes to be fertility symbols.

During this stage the Heel Stone was placed just beyond the entrance to this henge. It weighs about 35 tonnes and was brought to the site from Marlborough Down, about 22 miles (36 km) away – the nearest source for this type of stone.

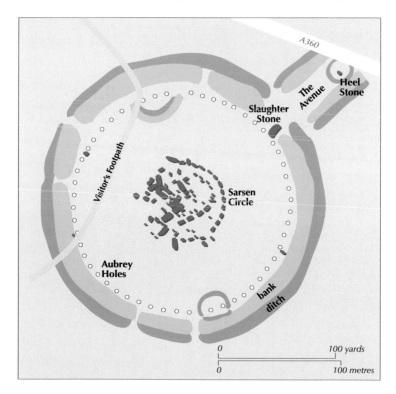

Stonehenge seen from the east showing the outer Sarsen Circle with remaining lintels and two larger sarsen trilithons.

The most northerly rising of the moon, which is called the 'major standstill', aligns exactly with a line connecting the Heel Stone with the centre of the circle.

2. In about 2,500 BC Stonehenge was rebuilt. This time the work was done entirely in stone. A new north-east axis was made to fit in with a broad embankment named the Avenue outside the ditch. The four Station Stones were positioned as a huge square and the legendary bluestones of Preseli were placed as two circles in the middle of the henge, each with an entrance looking straight along the Avenue.

3. Two hundred years later the final phase began which was to make Stonehenge even more impressive.

THE BLUESTONES

These stones with their soft grey-blue tones originated in the Preseli Hills in Pembrokeshire in Wales over 250 miles (400 km) away from Stonehenge. A 12th-century chronicler, Geoffrey of Monmouth, recorded that Merlin had used his magic to transport the stones which he called the Giant's Dance from Ireland to 'the mount of Ambrius' (which has been identified with Amesbury, very near Stonehenge). It is possible that the Preseli Hills were deemed sacred at the time as the remains of seven stone circles are to be found in the Preseli area.

The great sarsens were heaved upright and the top lintels were linked with vertical tongue-and-groove joints, each fixed onto its upright by a mortice-and-tenon joint. The stones were worked with hammers to an exact shape. The geometry of the lintels is accurately circular and level despite the sloping ground and it was designed to be on the alignment of the midsummer sun.

SARSEN STONES

Sarsen stones are large blocks of sandstone occurring naturally, scattered over the English chalk downs, probably the remnants of eroded sandstone beds. At Stonehenge they were shaped using heavy stone hammers. Further work in fashioning the mortice-and-tenon joints used to secure the lintels to the uprights was undertaken in the same way.

The bluestones were moved to form an oval between the Trilithon Horseshoe and the Sarsen Circle, plus a second horseshoe within the larger one.

4. In approximately 1,100 BC the Avenue was lengthened by a further 1.2 miles (2 km) so it met the River Avon. This can only be appreciated from the air as the ditches were later abandoned.

Today it is thought that the stones, which weigh about 5 tonnes (5000 kg), were transported both by land on massive rollers and sledges and by sea and river on rafts

– although a recent attempt in 2000 to recreate this feat failed completely. However it was done, it is obvious that it would require huge resources of manpower and, above all, planning and determination for the enterprise to be successful. Only a society that was united, at peace and capable of complex organisation could have achieved this.

SIGNIFICANCE OF THE SITE

Inevitably there are many theories as to what Stonehenge was for and how it was used. One theory has stood the test of time and is generally accepted to provide at least part of the answer to the puzzle.

Professor Alexander Thom proved that the alignments at Stonehenge were built to precise measurements so as to observe lunar and solar astronomy. He found that people who constructed the circles had a knowledge of mathematics that was only equalled a thousand years later in classical Greece.

Megalithic people were so attuned to their natural world that they could therefore predict the phases of the moon, eclipses of the sun and moon, and the rhythm of the seasons. Whether it was also a place of celebration and feasting or used for funeral and sacrificial rites is not known.

THE SURROUNDING MONUMENTS
WOODHENGE

Predating the major stone construction at Stonehenge is Woodhenge, 2 miles (3 km) to the north east, which dates to around 2,300 BC. It originally consisted of six concentric rings of timber posts probably covered with a roof. Facing its entrance and the rising sun, a shallow grave was uncovered that may be proof of human sacrifice. The grave contained the remains of girl aged three to four years old with her skull cleanly split in half by an axe.

THE CURSUS

A Neolithic monument just under a mile north of Stonehenge which extends for over a mile. Made of two straight banks and ditches it runs from east to west. The construction was given its name by 18th-century archaeologists who thought it was a race course for ancient British chariots. It is surrounded by many round barrows – Bronze Age burial mounds and long barrows are to be found extensively throughout the area. All this reinforces the idea that the whole area was a sacred site for remembrance and ceremonial.

Avebury

After the symmetry of Stonehenge this sprawling site with its enormous stones appears more primitive but on close inspection one can see that its builders were working to a precise measure and plan.

Avebury is an irregular henge with an outer boundary marked by an impressively deep ditch and bank. It was a colossal piece of building if one considers that it would have been excavated with only the most primitive of tools such as antler picks and rakes. Archaeologists have estimated that it would have taken as much as 1.5 million man hours to construct and transport the stones. The total area is an amazing 28.5 acres (11.5 ha).

Avebury: three of the colossal larger stones. The circles were constructed over 4,500 years ago.

The Great Circle of stones is the largest in Europe and it was first constructed in about 2,600 BC – over 4,500 years ago. Initially there were about 98 sarsens in the Great Circle which lies just within the henge ditch. Inside the Great Circle are two circles of stone, separate but of the same size: the Southern Circle once incorporated 29 stones and had a plinth at its heart. The Northern Circle was made up of two concentric rings, the inner of 12 stones and the outer 27. At its centre there remain two of the three sarsens that would have made a rectangular cove.

The sheer size of the stones and their irregular beauty are quite awe-inspiring, although it can be a confusing site to visit because the modern village of Avebury also stands inside these ancient remains. Many of the stones were broken up or buried by medieval farmers and villagers and their significance was not known to a wider world until John Aubrey came across Avebury in 1649. In 1723 the antiquary William Stukeley made drawings of the site in meticulous detail but it was not until the 1930s that it was properly excavated by Alexander Keiller and some of the stones re-erected. Stukeley had watched in horror as the local farmers and builders pushed over and broke up many of the stones to clear the land for ploughing and for re-use as building material.

> *'Avebury doeth as much exceed Stonehenge in grandeur as a Cathedral doth an ordinary Parish Church'*
> **John Aubrey**

Two avenues of stones emanated from the main circle, both one and half miles long (2.4 kilometres) and 15 metres (50 feet) wide. One avenue, remnants of which can still be seen, terminates at another stone circle to the south east of Avebury known as The Sanctuary. The other avenue, which now no longer exists, extended to the west.

View of Avebury showing a small part of the outer circle, the deep ditch and the village, much of which lies within the ancient workings.

SIGNIFICANCE OF THE SITE

Unlike Stonehenge the sarsens at Avebury were used in their natural state although it is very likely that they were chosen for their shapes – some are columnar, others have a square or triangular appearance. They may symbolise the male and female. They also came from the Marlborough Downs and it is thought that were once as many as 247 standing stones within the henge and 400 or more which formed the two avenues extending from the entrances of the circle. Most weigh about 15 tonnes but the huge Swindon Stone by the north entrance is 65 tonnes.

'that stupendous temple... at Abury... the most august work at this day upon the globe of the earth' **William Stukeley**

Stukeley believed that the site with its sinuous avenues was set out in the ancient form of a solar serpent: the Sanctuary circle was its head, the Kennet and Beckhampton Avenues the body which passed through the Avebury circle which symbolised the sun. Many ancient civilisations used the solar serpent to communicate the highest ideals of wisdom and creation.

The Beckhampton Avenue to the west of the henge is in the direction of Stonehenge – Avebury would have been in existence for over 700 years by the time the first sarsens were taken to Stonehenge.

THE SURROUNDING MONUMENTS

There are many more interesting traces of pre-Christian civilisation around Avebury.

WEST KENNET LONG BARROW

The barrow is a short distance from the main A4 road about a mile and half from

Avebury. It is one of the largest and best-preserved Neolithic long barrows in England and is dated to *c.* 3,700 BC. It was probably still in use until 2,000 BC. It is over 100 metres (328 ft) in length with a long stone passage off which lead four side chambers and a roomy end chamber. The remains in each chamber seemed to be differentiated by who was buried there – for example the west chamber was mainly for adult males, the south-west chamber for children. Much of the earthen mound has not yet been excavated. When the barrow ceased to be used, the people of the time took care to block it up by filling the entrance with earth and stones and erected three huge upright stones outside as an immovable barrier.

It is a very remarkable place especially inside where the workmanship can be fully appreciated. The remains of up to 46 people were found here when it was excavated. Possibly one of the last burials was of an old man whose throat had been pierced by an arrowhead.

SILBURY HILL

Along the road from West Kennet Long Barrow and dominating the landscape rises the green mound of ancient Silbury Hill.

The mystery of Silbury Hill remains unsolved. This giant earthwork rises above the road. It has never collapsed due to its internal retaining structure. It incorporates 250,000 cubic metres of earth and chalk and stands 40 metres high (130 ft) covering an area of 2.2 hectares (5 acres). Built about 5,000 years ago it is perfectly round with a flat summit which is 30 metres (100 ft) in diameter. Modern excavations have found nothing inside and have only served to weaken the structure which is currently being stabilised by infilling it with chalk.

Speculation about the hill will continue but it could have been a symbol of pregnancy or new life. One legend says that a solid gold horse and rider known as King Sil are buried there, another that the devil was going to empty a huge sack of earth on Marlborough, but was forced to drop it by the magic of the priests of Avebury.

Also near to Avebury is the Beckhampton Road Long Barrow, the large camp on Windmill Hill, the Sanctuary on Overton Hill and many round barrows scattered in the surrounding landscape.

Visitor Information

Opening times for Stonehenge

15 March–31 May	9.30 am – 6.00 pm
1 June–31 August	9.00 am – 7.00 pm
1 September–15 October	9.30 am – 6.00 pm
16 October–16 March	9.30 am – 4.00 pm
Boxing Day and New Year's Day	10.00 am – 4.00 pm

The site is open every day except Christmas Eve and Christmas Day.

How to get there

From Amesbury: 2 miles west on the junction of A303 and A344/360.

Avebury is on the A361 about 18 miles (28 km) north of Stonehenge.

From London Gatwick Airport: Take the M23 motorway and join the M25 motorway, following the signs for Heathrow Airport. From the M25, exit at junction 12 for the M3 motorway towards Basingstoke. Once on the M3 follow it to junction 8 signed A303 Andover. Continue on the A303 all the way until you reach a roundabout. Go straight over this and 2 miles on bear right onto the A344 and the car park is on the right hand side about 500 metres on.

From London Heathrow Airport: Follow signs to the M4 West. Continue for about 2 miles and come off at junction 4b onto the M25 South bound. Follow the signs for Gatwick Airport. From the M25, exit at junction 12 for the M3 motorway towards Basingstoke. Then follow the directions as above.

By train: The nearest train station to Stonehenge is Salisbury about 9.5 miles away. From London the trains depart from Waterloo Station.

By bus: Buses depart from Heathrow Airport and from Victoria Coach Station in the centre of London. The journey takes about 2 hours and there are three departures daily. Get off at Amesbury. From there you can either walk (about 2 miles), catch a local bus, or get a taxi. You can buy tickets on the coach, at the coach station, or from ticket agents for National Express.

General information on opening times: www.stonehenge.co.uk

Where to Stay

Marlborough or Salisbury are good bases for exploring the area.

Marlborough

Tourist Office 01672 512151

The Ivy House Hotel 01672 515333 www.ivyhousemarlborough.co.uk

Castle and Ball Hotel 01672 515201 www.castleandball.com

63 George Lane B & B 01672 512771

Salisbury

Tourist Office 01722 334956 www.visitsalisbury.com

Salisbury booking line 01271 336066

Best Western Red Lion Hotel 01722 323334 www.the-redlion.co.uk

Milford Hall Hotel 01722 417411 www.milfordhallhotel.com

B & B The Old Rectory 01722 502702 www.theoldrectory-bb.co.uk

Hilcott Farm House 01672 851372 www.hilcott.com

London and the South East

Canterbury Cathedral, St Augustine's Abbey
and St Martin's Church

Maritime Greenwich

Royal Botanic Gardens, Kew

Tower of London

Westminster Palace, Westminster Abbey
and St Margaret's Church

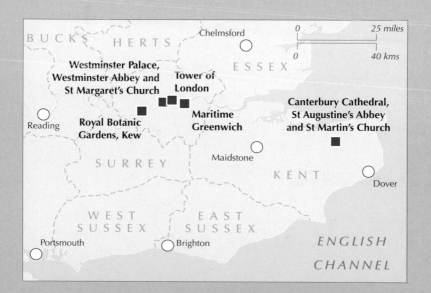

Opposite: Christ Church Cathedral at Canterbury by night.

Canterbury Cathedral, St Augustine's Abbey and St Martin's Church

A Spiritual Centre for the Anglican Church

Date of Inscription 1987

Why is this a World Heritage Site?

Canterbury has been an archiepiscopal seat for 1,500 years and the spiritual centre of the Church of England for nearly 500 years. Three separate buildings make up the World Heritage site: the modest St Martin's Church which is the oldest parish church in England kept in continuous use, the ruins of St Augustine's Abbey and the magnificent Christ Church Cathedral – all of which are milestones in the religious history of Great Britain.

Location

Canterbury is located in north-east Kent to the south of the Thames estuary in southern England.

BACKGROUND HISTORY

In 597 Pope Gregory the Great sent Augustine on a missionary expedition from Rome to England. The mission arrived at the court of the Anglo-Saxon king Ethelbert of Kent (c.560–616) whose Christian wife, Bertha, was the daughter of the king of the Franks. Ethelbert himself then converted to Christianity and gave Augustine and his companions authority to preach the gospel throughout the kingdom. Although the pope, having studied Roman documents about England, had intended that London and York should be the site of two archbishoprics, because Ethelbert's capital was in Canterbury, Augustine decided to establish the primary archbishopric there instead. On Christmas Day 597, 10,000 of King Ethelbert's subjects were baptised in what is referred to as the 'Miracle at Canterbury'. After his death, the king was canonised.

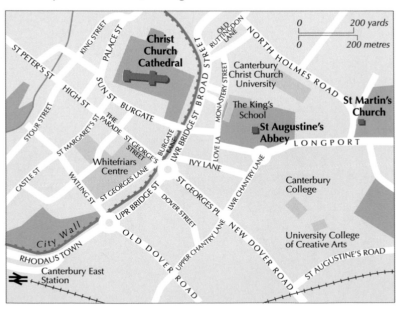

Canterbury Cathedral

Christ Church Cathedral is a major medieval building of vast size 168 metres (550 ft) long from east to west. The interior is one of the most beautiful architectural spaces of Early Gothic art in Europe.

Nothing remains of the cathedral established by Augustine in the 6th century. Following the conquest of England by the Normans, construction of a new cathedral was completed under the direction of Archbishop Lanfranc and was ready for use by the late 1070s. During the early 12th century the east end of the church was greatly enlarged. A fire in 1174 destroyed this enlarged east end which was rebuilt by the French master mason William of Sens in 1175–9 and his successor, simply called William the Englishman (who, despite his soubriquet, appears to have also hailed from France). William of Sens built the choir and eastern transepts on a plan dictated by the surviving crypt and aisle walls and may have designed the Trinity chapel and the tower-like Corona chapel although they were completed by William the Englishman.

William of Sens introduced the new French architectural style, first used in the building of the basilica of Saint-Denis outside Paris, which we now call Gothic. His innovatory use of highly polished dark Purbeck marble, giving decorative contrast inside the choir at Canterbury, was almost certainly

View of the exquisite 14th-century nave, by master mason Henry Yevele.

THOMAS BECKET (c. 1118–70)

After entering the service of Archbishop Theobald in 1145 Thomas Becket rose rapidly to become archdeacon of Canterbury. His talents attracted the attention of King Henry II who appointed Becket to the important post of Lord Chancellor, a position in which Becket was able to display his considerable abilities, all of which were marshalled in support of the king's policies even when those policies were in conflict with the church. Henry, who sought to curtail the power of the church, saw the loyal Becket as a steadfast ally and consequently chose him to succeed Theobald as archbishop of Canterbury when the incumbent died in 1162. To everyone's surprise, Becket's character then underwent a sea-change, he adopted a hairshirt, opposed the king's wishes at every opportunity and in 1164 fled the country in fear of retribution from an increasingly infuriated king.

In his French exile Becket led a studious and ascetic life but in his absence, the Archbishop of York had taken it upon himself to undertake the coronation of Henry's son as the 'Young King'. Becket saw this as an infringement of his privileges as primate of Canterbury. He came to an agreement with Henry for a return to England, whereupon he immediately excommunicated the Archbishop of York. This proved to be the last straw for Henry; he is reported to have said, 'Will no one rid me of this turbulent priest?' prompting four knights to travel to Canterbury where they murdered Becket in front of the altar of St Benedict in the cathedral. In penance for this bloody outrage Henry walked barefoot through Canterbury and was flogged by the monks. Becket was canonised three years later in 1173.

Becket's tomb, situated in the recently completed Trinity Chapel, soon became the greatest pilgrimage shrine in England (centuries later its continued importance is illustrated in *The Canterbury Tales*). Canterbury benefited enormously from the expenditure of numerous pilgrims. In 1538 Henry VIII declared Becket a traitor and his shrine was destroyed, perhaps in a belated attempt by the king to avenge his ancestor. Only a lighted candle now marks the spot where the shrine stood.

derived from the use of similar marble-like stone in cathedrals such as Tournai and Valenciennes in northern France.

The spacious Norman crypt, untouched by the fire of 1174, is well preserved. The highlight of the crypt is the carved capitals of the columns. These are the 'most ambitious, most finely conceived, and... best preserved Early Romanesque sculpture in the country' (John Newman *The Buildings of England* ed. Nikolaus Pevsner). In the chapels of the Holy Innocents and St Gabriel they are especially notable for lively scenes – for example one of animals playing musical instruments together with a dog and a mythical beast, the wyvern, fighting and another of jugglers.

A new nave, erected in 1377–1405, was probably designed by the great master mason Henry Yevele in early Perpendicular Gothic style featuring spectacular soaring vertical lines, replacing Lanfranc's earlier building. Finally the towers were completed, notably 'Bell Harry' 1494–1503 in late Perpendicular style. In the nave the filigree stone screen of the Chapel of Our Lady of the Undercroft is notable and in the Trinity Chapel, in the east end, lie the tombs of the Black Prince who died in 1376 and those of Henry IV and his queen, Joan of Navarre.

St Augustine's chair, or *Cathedra Augustini* is housed in the cathedral for the enthronements of archbishops. It is made of Purbeck marble and may date from as early as the 6th century.

The exquisite stained glass in the Trinity Chapel depicts the miracles worked

St Thomas Becket, Trinity Chapel Windows, c.1220.
The stained glass at Canterbury is one of the chief glories of the cathedral .

by the blood or intervention of St Thomas Becket. But this is only a part of the extensive medieval stained glass decorating the windows of Canterbury's east end (choir, presbytery, Corona, Trinity Chapel etc.). Canterbury has the greatest quantity of such glass in England with the exception of York Minster. However one of the great pleasures for the visitor to Canterbury is the proximity of much of this very beautiful glass to the viewer who can walk right up to enjoy the glazier's art.

An aerial view of the ruins of St Augustine's Abbey founded by the saint himself.

St Augustine's Abbey

Only the remains of this once great abbey can be seen today covering a substantial area east of the cathedral. It was founded in 597 by St Augustine as a Benedictine monastery and was intended to be a burial place for the Anglo-Saxon kings of Kent. The great crenellated gate of 1309 leads to the surviving stones which first suffered damage in an earthquake in 1382, then abandonment and ruin in 1538 during the Dissolution of the Monasteries. At the time of the Dissolution it had an income of £1733 and a magnificent library of over 2000 books – many of which would doubtless have been produced in the abbey's own scriptorium. After the monks had left, it became a palace for a succession of noble inhabitants. In the 17th century the great gardener, John Tradescant the elder, created a formal garden around it but it was finally abandoned after a great storm in 1703 caused havoc with the fragile structure of the old buildings. Today it is in the care of English Heritage.

St Martin's Church

This ancient church – which some believe to be the first church in England – stands east of the city well outside the old walls. It may be the church where Queen Bertha prayed before Augustine arrived in Canterbury. A simple structure, it includes some Roman brickwork from the 4th century. The Norman font is made of Caen stone decorated with a top row of intersected arches and intricate interlocking circles below. The dedication to St Martin is interesting as he was a popular French saint and bishop of Tours in 370.

Visitor Information

How to get there

By road

The M20 (M25 / M26) and M2 motorways provide easy links with London and its airports. Park & Ride in Canterbury is an efficient and easy service that goes straight into the heart of the city. You can park in one of the 1800 spaces across the three sites at New Dover Road, Sturry Road and Wincheap.

By Rail

Canterbury has two mainline stations, East and West, and is served by frequent trains to and from London, Charing Cross and London, Victoria, as well as to and from Dover and Ramsgate. If you travel by Eurostar to Ashford International there is a regular train service from there to Canterbury West.

National Rail Enquiries 08457 484950 From abroad 44 (0) 20 7278 5240
www.nationalrail.co.uk

By Bus and Coach

The district is well served by Stagecoach East Kent buses into Canterbury Bus Station. For timetable enquiries, please call 08456 00 22 99. National Express coaches travel regularly to and from Canterbury Bus Station to London, Victoria and Dover bus stations.

By Sea

There are ferry connections from Calais to Dover or you can take your car through the Channel Tunnel from Calais to Folkestone.

Opening times

The Cathedral

Open daily (apart from special events) www.canterbury-cathedral.org
Monday – Saturday 9.00 am – 5.00 pm: Sundays 12.30 – 2.30 pm and 4.30 – 5.30 pm

St Augustine's Abbey (managed by English Heritage)

1 April – 30 June Wednesday – Saturday 10.00 am – 5.00 pm
1 July – 31 August Daily 10.00 am – 6.00 pm
1 September – 31 March Sunday 11.00 am – 5.00 pm
Closed 24 – 26 December and 1 January

St Martin's Church

1 April – 30 September Tuesday, Thursday, Saturday 11.00 am – 6.00 pm
1 October – 30 March Tuesday, Thursday, Saturday 11.00 am – 3 pm

Tourist information

Contact Canterbury Information centre: www.canterbury.co.uk 01227 378100

Where to Stay

Canterbury Cathedral Lodge 01227 865350 www.canterburycathedrallodge.org
Ebury Hotel 01227 768433 www.eburyhotel.co.uk
The White House 01227 761836 www.sh-systems.co.uk

Maritime Greenwich

*Where Architecture and Science meet
at 0 Degrees Longitude*

Date of Inscription 1997

Why is this a World Heritage Site?	Greenwich is a unique assemblage of buildings that

together with the Royal Park bear witness to a period of unparalleled artistic, scientific and naval endeavour in the 17th and 18th centuries.

Location	The buildings are situated in the London borough of Greenwich which is situated a few miles to the south east of the City of London on the River Thames.

BACKGROUND HISTORY

Greenwich has been linked with the monarchy for many centuries. In the 8th century it was owned by Ethelrada, niece of Alfred the Great. In the 15th century the estate was the property of Duke Humphrey, brother of Henry V, who bought the manor of Greenwich from the Carthusians of West Sheen. He called it Bella Court and it housed his collection of rare books, a library that was later to form the core of the Bodleian Library in Oxford. Later Henry VI (1422–61) built the Palace of Placentia and lived there with his wife, Margaret of Anjou. Henry VII built extensive additions and three later Tudor monarchs were born at the palace – Henry VIII, Mary I and Elizabeth I.

There is an old oak tree in Greenwich Park known as Queen Elizabeth's oak where she is reputed to have played as a child. The oak collapsed in 1991 but a remnant of its base remains. In 1613 James I (1603–25) gave the palace to his wife, Anne of Denmark, but, finding it too old-fashioned for her taste, she commissioned the notable architect Inigo Jones to build the Queen's House to its south. During the Civil War between Charles I and his Parliament, the Tudor palace was used as a biscuit factory after which it gradually fell into disrepair until it was demolished.

THE QUEEN'S HOUSE

The focus of the present Greenwich ensemble of buildings is the classically proportioned Palladian house (see below) designed in 1616 by Inigo Jones initially for Anne of Denmark. It is now in use as an art gallery showing part of the

National Maritime Museum's collection which ranges from Tudor portraits to 20th-century paintings and includes some fine Canalettos.

Inspired by the architecture of Renaissance Italy, the Queen's House features a hall in the form of a perfect cube with a gallery around the upper floor, a tulip staircase and a loggia which overlooks the park. Jones' design was a complete break from the asymmetrical, heavily decorative style of Tudor architecture and became a direct inspiration for later grand houses and villas all over Britain for the next 200 years. The building was completed in 1635 for its second queen, Henrietta Maria, the wife of Charles I.

THE OLD ROYAL NAVAL COLLEGE

It was Charles II (1660–85) who decided to pull the old Tudor palace down and build a splendid new Baroque palace for himself starting with the King Charles Court designed by John Webb. It was completed in the reign of William and Mary as a naval hospital and the three other royal courts added by the greatest architects of the day – Wren, Hawksmoor, Vanbrugh and James 'Athenian' Stuart. In the 19th century it became an infirmary for the pensioners of the Royal Navy before the establishment of the Royal Naval College. Following the College's move in the 1990s a university campus was formed to house Trinity College of Music and the University of Greenwich.

A view of one of the colonnades which grace the Baroque Royal Naval College.

The magnificent Baroque Painted Hall with its sumptuously decorated ceiling is where Nelson's body lay in state after the battle of Trafalgar. It is open to the public as is the Chapel across Grand Square with its glorious Rococo plasterwork. The Pepys building contains a Visitor Centre and Greenwich tourist information centre.

'The most stately procession of buildings we possess'
Professor Sir Charles Reilly

THE NATIONAL MARITIME MUSEUM

The museum was opened to the public by King George VI in 1937. It is housed in the Queen's House and former Royal Hospital School. In the late 20th century it was extended to form Neptune Court which is now an exciting exhibition space

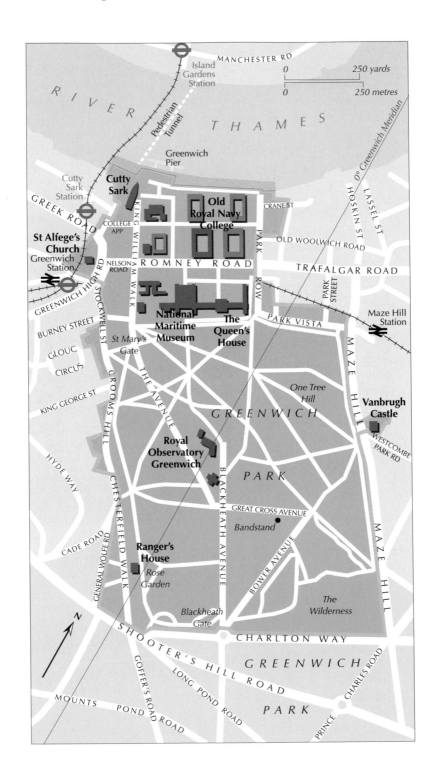

A view of the Royal Observatory from Greenwich Park. The orange time-ball drops every 24 hours at 1.00 pm. The Prime Meridian lies nearby.

celebrating Britain's seafaring heritage, including the stories of naval battles, great explorers and adventurers, all of which draw on the museum's collection of almost 2.5 million items.

ROYAL OBSERVATORY

The Observatory sits on the brow of Greenwich Hill and dominates the landscape. It was built at the behest of Charles II in 1675 to further studies in astronomy and navigation. Probably designed by Sir Christopher Wren, the first Astronomer Royal, John Flamsteed, lived and worked here. Flamsteed, a deeply religious man, made over 20,000 observations, despite the fact that he suffered from ill health, plotting the moon's orbit and the positions of the stars. He worked closely with Isaac Newton but hated his successor Edmund Halley, possibly because Halley was a noted atheist.

The observatory is furnished with clocks and telescopes and includes John Harrison's timepieces from the 18th century which finally helped to solve the problems of establishing longitude at sea.

The octagonal room was used by Flamsteed as a workplace and also by the Royal Society for meetings and dinners. It is surmounted by the famous time-ball which drops to indicate Greenwich Mean Time every 24 hours at 1.00 pm [See also Edinburgh page 214]. Nearby, visitors can stand across the Prime Meridian with one foot in the eastern hemisphere and the other in the west.

'the most exact care and diligence to rectifying the tables of the Motions of the Heavens, and the Places of the fixed stars, so as to find out the most desired Longitude at Sea, for perfecting the art of Navigation.'

King Charles II on the reasons for building the Royal Observatory

THE PRIME MERIDIAN

The Royal Observatory is the source of the Prime Meridian, Longitude 0° 0' 0". Every place on the Earth is measured in terms of its distance east or west from this line. The line itself divides the eastern and western hemispheres of the Earth – just as the Equator divides the northern and southern hemispheres.

The Prime Meridian is defined by the position of the large 'Transit Circle' telescope in the Observatory's Meridian Building. This was built by Sir George Biddell Airy, the 7th Astronomer Royal, in 1850. The cross-hairs in the eyepiece of the Transit Circle precisely define Longitude 0° for the world.

The Greenwich Meridian was chosen as the Prime Meridian of the World in 1884. Forty-one delegates from 25 nations met in Washington DC for the International Meridian Conference. The Paris Meridian, established in the early 1800s by the French astronomer François Arago, was the other major contender and France abstained from the voting at the conference. France retained the Paris Meridian for the purposes of timekeeping until 1911 and until 1914 for navigational calculations.

GREENWICH PARK

This is London's oldest enclosed park. Charles II commissioned a formal design inspired by the great French landscape gardener André Le Nôtre using sweet chestnuts and elms in straight avenues aligned on the Queen's House. Little of this original planting now remains although a few chestnuts survive, the elms having recently succumbed to Dutch elm disease. Blackheath Avenue also survives from this scheme but today the park more closely resembles the 18th-century ideal of English informal landscaping.

BUILDINGS AROUND THE PARK
VANBRUGH CASTLE

Designed by Sir John Vanbrugh, the architect of Blenheim Palace, who also worked on the Royal Naval College, it was modelled on the Bastille in Paris where Vanbrugh was imprisoned on charges of spying in 1690–92. Sir John lived there from 1719–26. Today it has been converted into apartments.

RANGER'S HOUSE

Built in 1700–20 this is a handsome seven-bayed building in brick (rear view, right, seen from the Rose Garden in Greenwich Park) which houses the Wernher Collection of Renaissance objets d'art, antique furniture and Georgian art. It is open to the public.

The Old Royal Naval College looking north west across the Thames towards the towers of the financial centre of Canary Wharf.

Nearby Sites

St Alfege's Church

The parish church of Greenwich is one of the masterpieces of Sir Nicholas Hawksmoor, built in 1711–14.

The *Cutty Sark*

The famous tea-clipper was built in 1869 and was once the fastest ship in the world. It is berthed in a special dry-dock and maintained as a museum. Restoration work necessitated its closure in 2006 but in May 2007 disaster struck when a fire broke out. It has since been announced that the *Cutty Sark* will reopen in 2010 thanks to a donation of £3.3m from the shipping magnate Sammy Ofer.

Please see www.cuttysark.org.uk for updates. Adjacent to the ship is the *Cutty Sark* Pavilion visitor centre.

Where to stay

Greenwich Tourist Information Centre 0870 608 2000
www.greenwich.gov.uk/tourism email tic@greenwich.gov.uk

Novotel, London Greenwich 020 8312 6900 www.novotel.com

Devonport House Hotel 0870 609 1143 www.devere.co.uk

Number 16 B &B 020 8853 4337 www.st-alfeges.co.uk

Visitor Information

How to get there

Consult www.greenwichwhs.org.uk

By rail

Trains leave from Charing Cross, Waterloo East and London Bridge to Greenwich.

Docklands Light Railway

Nearest DLR station is Cutty Sark for Maritime Greenwich.

Underground

The Jubilee Line does not serve central Greenwich but provides excellent connections involving just one change. To reach central Greenwich from the Jubilee Line change at Canary Wharf for the DLR to Cutty Sark Station.

Bus

Numbers 188, 177, 180, 199, 286 and 386.

By River

Pleasure cruises are operated by:

Catamaran Cruisers / Bateaux London: 020 7987 1185
City Cruises: 020 7740 0400
Thames River Services: 020 7930 4097
Thames Clippers offer a fast river service: 0870 781 5049 www.thamesclippers.com
This is a daily river commuter service, approximately every 15 minutes on 220 seater vessels. This serves a number of business locations along the river with a timetable oriented to business users. The service calls at these piers: Embankment, Blackfriars, Bankside, London Bridge, Tower, Canary Wharf, Greenland, Masthouse Terrace, Greenwich, QE2 and Royal Arsenal, Woolwich.

Disabled access

Consult the river operator for full details. Europe's first Ramp Rider is installed at Greenwich Pier. This improves access for wheelchair users getting on and off boats at Greenwich at low tide.

By car

Recommended routes:

From the north use M25, M11, A406 (direction London East), A12, Blackwall Tunnel.
From the south use M25, A2 (a fast route straight to Greenwich).
From Dover it is best to use the A2, M2, A2 route direct to Greenwich.
From Channel Tunnel use M20, M25, A2.

If you are using satellite navigation, use the following postcodes:

SE10 9NF for the Museum car park.

SE10 8QY for the Blackheath Gate which leads to the Royal Observatory.

Opening times

The National Maritime Museum, Queen's House and the Royal Observatory are open daily from 10.00 am to 5.00 pm Closed 24–26 December.
The Prime Meridian courtyard is open until 8.00 pm in the summer.

Old Royal Naval College: Grounds open daily
Painted Hall and Chapel: Open daily 10.00 am – 5.00 pm

Cutty Sark Pavilion Visitor centre: Sunday, Monday and Tuesday 11.00 am – 5.00 pm

Opposite: A view of the Palm House at Kew with summer bedding.

Royal Botanic Gardens, Kew

The Celebrated Repository of over 40,000 plants

Date of Inscription 2003

Why is this a World Heritage Site?

These beautiful and historic gardens have long been a delightful amenity for Londoners and are enjoyed by about a million visitors a year.

Kew Gardens satisfy several of the criteria necessary for inclusion. From their inception in the 18th century, the gardens have been a botanic resource for the advancement of science and for 'economic exchange' when species were collected from all over the world and then sent elsewhere to further other country's economies – for instance the start-up of the rubber industry in Malaya. In this instance seeds which were received from Amazonian rubber trees were germinated at Kew and then sent to Malaysia and Sri Lanka.

Since their creation in 1759, the gardens have made a significant contribution to the study of plant diversity and economic botany. They are notable for the exceptional richness of their plant collections which are important for teaching, medicine and conservation. And just as the plants themselves enriched the world, the style of landscaping and the architectural features of the gardens created by great innovators such as Charles Bridgeman, William Kent and Lancelot 'Capability' Brown had an international influence.

Location

The Royal Botanic Gardens are situated on the south bank of the River Thames in the Borough of Richmond, south west of London, and extend over 132 hectares (300 acres).

HISTORY

In 1772 two royal estates were combined: Richmond (the western half of today's gardens) and Kew (which took up the eastern side). Three other estates from private residences and their gardens were also included. The gardens are 'royal' because these estates were owned by the royal family. King George II and Queen Caroline lived at Ormonde Lodge on the Richmond estate and their son, Prince Frederick, leased the Kew estate. Queen Charlotte used the services of two well-known landscape gardeners, Charles Bridgeman and William Kent, noted for their then innovative approach to the art of gardening.

Prince Frederick died in 1751 (it was his son who was to become the future George III) and Augusta, his widow, started a modest botanic garden originally for medicinal plants. In this she was helped by Lord Bute and William Chambers who was a devotee of the fashion for 'chinoiserie' and designed the pagoda in 1761.

On his accession in 1760, George III inherited the Richmond estate and used

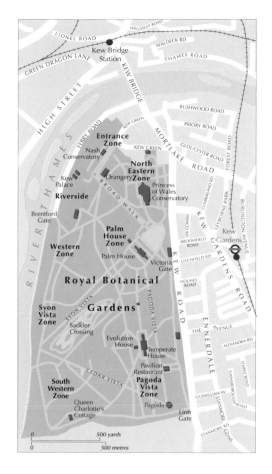

Capability Brown to create a landscaped park. But it was Sir Joseph Banks, fellow of the Royal Society and collector of flora and fauna on Captain Cook's famous first voyage to Australia, who set Kew on the path to becoming one of the world's great botanical collections. He became the unofficial head of the gardens in 1773 and shared with the king a determination to furnish them with exotic as well as native plants. Plant hunters were dispatched all over the world to bring back new species and Kew became the centre of 'botanic economics' for Great Britain and her colonies.

In 1802 the wall between the two parts of the gardens was taken down. After the deaths of Joseph Banks and George III, the gardens fell into decline but they were saved from closure and handed over to the state in 1840. The appointment of Sir William Hooker in 1841 as the first official director inspired revitalisation of the gardens.

A Visit to the Gardens
The Entrance Zone

The most historic part of Kew is near to the Main Gate – where Princess Augusta planted the original Botanic Garden. To the right is the Nash Conservatory which came from Buckingham Palace and the Georgian Orangery which was built in 1761 and is now a restaurant. Next door to the modern shop is a children's interactive play area known as Climbers and Creepers.

The ice house is surrounded by the Winter Garden which is best on a cold grey day with its colourful scented shrubs. One of the oldest trees in Kew, the Pagoda Tree with its gnarled trunk, is nearby, as well as the Lilac Garden for springtime and the Secluded Garden designed to appeal to all the senses with perfumed plants and a running stream.

JOSEPH BANKS (1743–1820)

A rich man with a passion for botany, Joseph Banks dedicated his life to science and the world of plants. After studying at Oxford University he travelled to Newfoundland and Labrador collecting plants and other specimens. In 1768 he joined Captain Cook's expedition to chart the undiscovered lands of the South Pacific aboard the *Endeavour*. He brought back many specimens and his account of his discoveries in the South Seas, New Zealand and Australia enthralled the European scientific community. His primary interest was in plants which could be used for practical purposes. In 1778 he was elected President of the Royal Society – a position he held for the rest of his life. His collection accounted for 110 new genera and 1,300 new species of which some 75 bear his name.

THE NORTH-EASTERN ZONE

This part of the gardens is nearest to Kew Bridge and was once a series of small houses with their gardens. Many of the buildings are used for offices or housing. There are several separate gardens including the Aquatic Garden, the Grass Garden, the Duke's Garden, Specimen Beds and the Rock Garden. The highlight here is the Princess of Wales Conservatory named in honour of Augusta, Princess of Wales, the founder of the gardens, which was opened by her modern equivalent Diana, Princess of Wales in 1987. Under its glass are 10 different climatic zones all controlled by computer. Most prominent are the two zones of the Dry Tropics and the Wet Tropics displaying the plants that thrive in these habitats.

THE PALM HOUSE ZONE

The Palm House is probably Kew's most loved feature. It was designed by the architects Richard Turner and Decimus Burton and is undoubtedly among the finest 19th-century glasshouses still standing. It contains one of the world's largest

The elegant Palm House, erected in 1844-48, is the most iconic building at Kew.

collections of palms from tropical rain forests and also tropical plants noted for their economic importance. To step into the humid heat of the Palm House on an English winter's afternoon is certainly one of Kew's greatest pleasures.

The Palm House terrace always has colourful bedding displays which alter with the seasons. Behind the Palm House is the classic Rose Garden with 54 beds of roses that are at their best in the months of July and August. Beyond the Palm House pond and terrace is the pleasantly landscaped Woodland Garden with its Temple of Aeolus.

Adjacent to the Palm House is the Waterlily House, another listed glasshouse built by Richard Turner in 1852.

Pagoda Vista Zone

The octagonal Pagoda was built in 1762. Its ten storeys are nearly 50 metres high (163 ft). Originally the Pagoda had a dramatic roof featuring 80 gilded wooden dragons but they have not survived the ravages of time.

The Pagoda was designed by William Chambers at the height of his 'Chinese period' in the 1760s .

After the Pagoda, the Temperate House is central to this part of the gardens. It is now the world's largest surviving Victorian glass structure and bears all the hallmarks of the genius of Decimus Burton. Contemporary planting is laid out in geographical zones and features beautiful and rare plants. These include endangered species which are being propagated for reintroduction to their native habitats and many plants of economic importance such as a citrus collection, quinine, tea and the date palm. Temperate plants from the Americas are found as well as exotic Australian species, some of which were first bought to Kew by Joseph Banks. One of the last surviving specimens of a cycad, *Encephalartos woodii*, grows here and it is hoped that it might in time bring forth a seed cone.

William Chambers (1723–96)

Sir William Chambers designed many of the buildings in Kew. Those still standing include the Pagoda, the Orangery, the Ruined Arch, the Temple of Bellona and the Temple of Aeolus. Others such as a mosque, a Palladian bridge and a menagerie have not stood the test of time. He was born in Sweden of Scottish descent and worked for the Swedish East India Company for whom he travelled to Bengal and Canton. His influence in Britain began when he was appointed architectural tutor to the future George III and as architect at Kew by Princess Augusta. His many other triumphs in the world of architecture include the building of Somerset House in London and the design of the gilded coach which is still used by the monarch for coronations today.

Adjacent to the Temperate House is a new structure – the Evolution House where the visitor is taken through imaginative displays showing 3,500 million years of plant evolution.

SOUTH-WESTERN ZONE

This is a conservation area boasting one of London's few bluebell woods which border Queen Charlotte's picturesque cottage with its thatch and rustic features. It was once used by the royal family for picnics and family outings. New additions to the woodland include a walk-through Badger Sett, a Dipping Pond, a Gravel Pit and a Loggery for stag beetles.

THE RHIZOTRON AND XSTRATA TREETOP WALKWAY

In the spring of 2008 an exciting new feature opened in the gardens. The entrance to the Rhizotron is fashioned to look like a crack in the ground and visitors can look at the natural world beneath the trees. The path then rises 18 metres (60 feet) into the air where the Treetop Walkway gives a stunning view of Kew Gardens and the London skyline whilst wandering through the lush green canopies of mature sweet chestnuts (planted by Capability Brown in the 1770s), oaks and limes. There is full wheelchair access and a solid viewing platform.

SYON VISTA ZONE

The wide Syon Vista looks across the Thames to a view of Syon House on its opposite bank. This part of the gardens owes its character to the mid-19th century design of William Nesfield. The lake adjacent to the vista is an artificial one and the spoil which was dug out when it was created became the mound on which the

Temperate House stands. The best time to see the lake is in the autumn when the surrounding plants blaze with seasonal colours which are reflected in the calm waters.

Following in the footsteps of Capability Brown who preferred curves and 'the sinuous line of grace', a new addition, the Sackler Crossing, opened in 2006. It was designed by the architect John Pawson and snakes across the lake. Black granite and bronze have been used in its construction – natural components which will age well. The crossing is set low and in some lights the bridge looks as if it is almost part of the water.

The graceful Sackler Crossing, designed by John Pawson, was opened in 2006.

The Rhododendron Dell features over 700 different specimens including hybrids unique to Kew.

WESTERN ZONE

This area of the gardens is easily accessed by visitors who arrive at Kew through the Brentford Gate. It has three key areas each with special planting. The Bamboo Garden first planted in 1891–2 with its traditional Japanese Minka house has the largest collection of bamboos in Britain.

The Azalea Garden is planted in two concentric circles with the plants arranged in date order from the earliest hybrids in the 1820s to the latest varieties from the Netherlands and America. But the loveliest part of the garden is the Rhododendron Dell which is one of the largest earthworks in Kew. This valley was made in the late 18th century by Capability Brown and the ha-ha he designed still marks the boundary between the gardens and the banks of the Thames. The rhododendrons came later in the 1850s and there are now over 700 specimens which flourish in late May although there is colour from November to August.

RIVERSIDE

This zone features the oldest building in Kew, the Dutch House of 1631, now named Kew Palace. It was erected on the banks of the Thames for a merchant of Dutch origin in red brick. At the back of the house is the formal Queen's Garden, a parterre design of 1959 which only contains plants grown in England during and before the 17th century.

The Bee Garden is much more informal and features many hives set amongst flowers popular with bees.

WHERE TO STAY

The Inn at Kew Gardens 020 8940 2220 www.theinnatkewgardens.com
Richmond Hill Hotel 020 8940 2247 www.foliohotels.com/richmondhill
11 Leyborn Park B & B 020 8948 1615 www.stay-in-kew.com
For central London see page 91

Visitor Information

How to get there

By Underground

Kew Gardens Station on the District Line.

By Train

Silverlink Metro Train Services: North Woolwich, West Ham, Stratford, Highbury and Islington, West Hampstead, Willesden Junction, Gunnersbury, Kew Gardens, Richmond.

South West Trains: London Waterloo, Clapham Junction, Putney, Barnes,, Chiswick, Kew Bridge, then to Brentford.

By Bus

Several buses go directly to the Gardens or stop at either of the two nearby railway stations, Kew Bridge and Kew Gardens.

No. 65: Ealing Broadway Station, South Ealing Station (Picadilly Line from Heathrow), Brentford, Kew Green (for Main Gate), Kew Road (for Victoria Gate), Lion Gate, Richmond.

No. 237: Hounslow, Isleworth, Brentford, Kew Bridge – terminates Shepherds Bush Green.

No. 267: Twickenham, Isleworth, Brentford, Kew Bridge, Gunnersbury, Hammersmith.

No. 391: Richmond, Kew Gardens Station, Kew Green (for Main Gate), Kew Bridge, Stamford Brook, Hammersmith, Fulham Broadway.

Travelling by Car

Kew Gardens are well signposted from all the major local roads. The South Circular (A205) passes the north-east corner of Kew Gardens and Kew Road (A307) forms the eastern border. If coming from the west on the M4 (leave at Junction 2) or A4 take the A205 to the right (at the major Chiswick roundabout (A4 / A406 / A205) and follow the A205 across the River Thames at Kew Bridge.

If coming from the North Circular or from London on the A4 take the A205 southwards at the Chiswick roundabout. Immediately over the bridge turn right into Kew Green and park on the roadside in a permitted place or head into the car park accessed via Ferry Lane on the river side of Kew Green.

Coming from the south or west on the A316 or M3 motorway (which becomes the A316) turn left at the Richmond roundabout onto Kew Road (A307). You will see the Pagoda and flagpole to your left – park in a permitted place, alongside the Gardens, on Kew Road.

Coming from the south on the South Circular Road you will pass Kew Retail Park; go under a railway bridge. Shortly afterwards, you will arrive at traffic lights where the A307 joins from the left, go slowly through the junction and immediately turn left into Kew Green (NOT back left into the A307 – it is a 'no left turn' junction).

Parking for cars

There is a car park near the Brentford Gate, reached via Ferry Lane off Kew Green near the Main Gate. It will take about 300 cars so parking is limited. It costs £5.00 for a full day throughout the year. The car park closes half an hour after the gardens close so is only suitable for day visitors.

Several dedicated parking bays are available for disabled drivers, for whom parking is free at all times. There are three further disabled parking bays adjacent to Main Gate on Kew Green. Free parking is available on Kew Road (A307) after 10.00 am every morning.

Opening times

Kew Gardens are open every day except Christmas Eve and Christmas Day.

1 April – 2 September: Mon – Friday, 9.30 am – 6.00 pm, Saturday & Sunday, 9.30 am – 7.00 pm
3 September – 27 October: 9.30 am – 5.30 pm; 28 October – 8 February: 9.30 am – 3.45 pm

Opposite: The Norman White Tower at the heart of the Tower of London.

Tower of London

London's Historic Fortress

Date of Inscription 1988

Why is this a World Heritage Site?

A stalwart symbol of state power and the might of the monarchy, the Tower of London has dominated the London skyline for many centuries. It was built by William the Conqueror both to protect the capital and to provide him with a secure stronghold. The iconic White Tower is a perfectly preserved example of military architecture and its design became a blueprint for other Norman fortresses erected throughout the kingdom. However, the Tower is famous not just for its architecture but for its many memorable historical associations.

Location

Now in the heart of the modern city, the Tower of London was built in a strategic position on the north bank of the river just downstream from London Bridge. The Normans built over existing Roman fortifications and incorporated the Roman wall and defensive turrets on the riverside. Now it is one of London's major tourist attractions not just because of its architecture but as a result of its links with many seminal events in Britain's history – a place where princes and princesses were imprisoned or murdered and where queens were executed. To add to the spectacle it is patrolled by Yeoman Warders – the 'Beefeaters' – in their red, blue and gold uniforms. It is also the repository for the magnificent Crown Jewels.

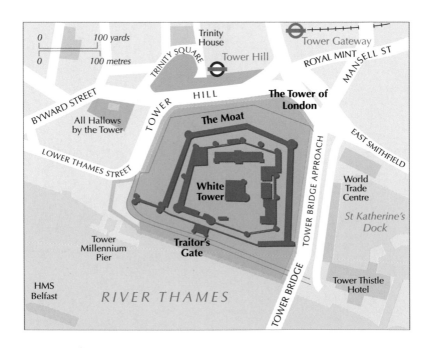

HISTORY
NORMAN BEGINNINGS

After his victory at the Battle of Hastings in 1066, William the Conqueror was crowned king at Westminster Abbey on Christmas Day of that same year. His first concern was to fortify London and protect his new capital but also to put on a show of strength to the 'vast and fickle population' of London.

Speed was of the essence so he had an earth-and-timber keep built on top of an artificial mound in the south-east angle of the ancient Roman city walls which commanded the city on its most vulnerable seaward side. On the north west a ditch and a palisade protected the yard. The site also included St Peter's church. Ten years later construction began on the massive keep, the White Tower.

'A most famous and goodly Citadell, encompassed round with thicke and strong walles, full of loftie and stately Turrets, fensed with a broad and deep ditch, furnished also with an armorie or magazine of warlicke munition, and other buildings beside: so it resembleth a big towne.'

William Camden, 1610

THE WHITE TOWER

Gundulf, the bishop of Rochester, designed this ambitious building. The walls are 28 metres high (90ft) and 4–5 metres thick (15ft) built of Kentish rag, bolstered by stone from Caen in Normandy brought over by sea and thence upriver. The White Tower (so called because its walls were whitewashed) became the centre of a complex of fortifications, courtyards and buildings which extend over 7.3 hectares (18 acres). The *Anglo-Saxon Chronicle* commented in 1097 that 'many shires whose labour was due to London were hard pressed because of the wall that they built around the Tower'.

The Tower is an example par excellence of the royal Norman castle in the late 11th century and served as a prototype for the many stone keeps which were subsequently built in stone including Colchester, Rochester, Hedingham, Norwich and Carisbrooke Castle on the Isle of Wight.

Apart from the decorative turrets built in the 16th century and the surrounds to the doors and windows, the original building has been preserved. It is probably one of the largest and most complete secular buildings of 11th-century Europe to survive.

THE MEDIEVAL TOWER

Medieval kings added many more buildings to the Tower, using it not only as a fortress but as a prison and a royal palace. During Richard the Lionheart's reign (1189–99) a curtain wall was begun and the Bell Tower built. King Henry III (1216–72) extended the royal apartments, built two new towers on the waterfront (the Wakefield and the Lanthorn) and rebuilt the chapel dedicated to St Peter ad Vincula. He also had the White Tower whitewashed within and without. In 1238 a massive curtain wall on the north, west and eastern sides was begun, reinforced

View of the Tower's outer defences showing the complexity of concentric additions.

by nine new towers and surrounded by a moat. The king also had a walled orchard, a vineyard and gardens planted within the inner walls.

Henry's successor Edward I (1272–1307) paid over £21,000 to fill in the moat and create another curtain wall to enclose the existing outer curtain which made the Tower into England's largest and strongest castle. Around this a new moat was created which was about 50 metres (160 ft) wide. (see pages 144-150 for Edward I's similar fortifications in Wales where defences were arranged concentrically). The moat was stocked with pike from Cambridge.

In 1281, between June and December, the Beauchamp Tower was erected and like his father, Edward again rebuilt the Chapel of St Peter ad Vincula. A branch of the Royal Mint was established in these secure surroundings (remaining there until the 19th century).

THE WARDROBE

This was the term for a place of safekeeping and at the Tower jewels, weaponry, wax and spices were kept in the Great Wardrobe. Later this devolved into the Armoury and the Board of Ordnance. As there was no standing army in medieval times these organisations were responsible for the procuring and storing of munitions which included armour, guns and pikes and heavier weapons such as cannon – the ordnance. Gunpowder and its ingredients were stored and made up here. Not only were weapons and guns tested and assembled but many staff of the Ordnance were housed within the Tower. In the 18th century military map makers were based at the Tower and later, civilian maps, the famous Ordnance Survey series, began to be published based in part on their work.

THE PEASANT'S REVOLT 1381

Richard II and his family and councellors took refuge in the Tower when almost 20,000 peasants led by Wat Tyler, John Ball and Jack Straw marched on London. When the king left the Tower to meet the mob's leaders as arranged, about 400 of them rushed into the fortress and ransacked the royal apartments. Some even had the temerity to 'arrogantly lay and sat and joked on the king's bed, whilst several asked the king's mother… to kiss them'. The Queen Mother was rescued but others including the Archbishop of Canterbury were seized and summarily killed on Tower Hill.

THE WAR OF THE ROSES 1455–87

The holding of the Tower was key to the two warring sides – the Houses of York and Lancaster. Tournaments and celebratory feasts were held there but for the vanquished it became a grim place of murder and execution. Henry VI was killed on 27 May 1471 while at his prayers in the Wakefield Tower and Edward IV's brother, George, Duke of Clarence was imprisoned and reputedly drowned 'in a butt of sweet wine'.

THE PRINCES IN THE TOWER

'Then, all the others being removed from them, this Miles Forest and John Dighton about midnight (the children lying in their beds) came into the chamber and suddenly lapped them up among the clothes so bewrapped them and entangled them, keeping down by force the featherbed and pillows hard unto their mouths, that within a while, smothered and stifled, their breath failing, they gave up to God their innocent souls into the joys of heaven, leaving to the tormentors their bodies dead in the bed.' **Sir Thomas More's account of the murder of the two Princes in the Tower**

THE ROYAL MENAGERIE

In Henry III's reign a strange assortment of animals was kept in the Tower. There were three leopards sent by the Holy Roman Emperor to match those on the royal arms of England, a polar bear from the king of Norway (safely chained it was allowed to catch fish for its supper in the river) and an elephant which was a gift from the king of France. There were also lions, bears, tigers and mastiffs – lion skulls have been found and radiocarbon dated to between 1285 and 1385. In the 19th century all the remaining animals were sent to be housed in London Zoo.

The most notorious captives were the sons of Edward IV: Edward V and his younger brother, Richard, Duke of York, who after entering the Tower's grim portals were never seen again. It is alleged that their uncle, Richard III (1483–85) had them murdered as they stood between him and the throne of England. Excavations in 1674 revealed the pathetic remains of two children in a box. Workmen threw the remains on a rubbish heap, but they were later recovered when it was realised that the bones might be those of the two princes. They were gathered up and placed in an urn which Charles II ordered to be interred in Westminster Abbey.

In 1933 the bones were exhumed and examined before being replaced in the urn and returned to the Abbey vault. The re-examination showed the skeletal remains to be of two boys, one aged about 10 and the other about 12.

THE TUDORS

Henry VII and Henry VIII were the last monarchs to improve the royal apartments in the Tower for themselves and their household although it was by then not a principal residence and was mainly used for ceremonial occasions. The Great Chamber was refurbished with a new roof and floor to make it a suitable place for the coronation of Anne Boleyn in 1533. In an unhappy twist, the same chamber was then used for her trial in 1536 and she was imprisoned in the Tower until her execution just two weeks later on 19 May. However, by the time of the accession of James I in 1603 the royal rooms and ceremonial areas were dilapidated and not fit for use. Charles II could not stay the night before his coronation but started his procession to the abbey from the Tower gates thereby once more asserting its traditional importance.

17TH–19TH CENTURIES

In this period many of the medieval buildings were pulled down and new warehouses built for an Ordnance store, offices and lodgings for officials and workers. A pair of splendid houses were built between 1699 and 1701 for the Surveyor and Clerk of the Ordnance on the site now used for the HQ of the Royal Regiment of Fusiliers.

During the reign of George I (1714–27) the Drawing Room for the Ordnance was established for the purpose of training military surveyors and draughtsmen and the production, in the first instance, of military maps of Scotland. It was not until 1841 that the Ordnance Survey left the Tower.

THE DUKE OF WELLINGTON

In 1826 the duke was appointed to be Constable of the Tower, a post he held until his death in 1852. With typical energy he had the moat drained of its noxious silt and water, a new barracks built within its walls (destroyed in the Second World War) and ordered the renewal of some defences especially to the west and north ramparts. The duke saw a possible threat from popular movements such as the Chartists.

THE 20TH CENTURY

Conservation and restoration of the medieval fortress were the main priorities during the 20th century. Once again it was used as a place of imprisonment when the Irish nationalist, Sir Roger Casement, was held in St Thomas's Tower in 1916 during his trial for treason. Considerable damage was caused to the Tower and its buildings during 1940 when over 50 incendiary devices fell on the area – all luckily narrowly missing the White Tower.

Hitler's deputy, Rudolph Hess, was placed in the Queen's House for four days in May 1941 and the spy Joseph Jakobs was shot here on 14 August, 1941. The last reported prisoners were the notorious Kray brothers who were briefly held there in 1952 for desertion from the army.

The Crown Jewels and the most treasured items in the Royal Armouries were moved to secret locations during the Second World War and the basement of the White Tower was used as an air raid shelter. In 1994 Queen Elizabeth II opened the new Jewel House.

VISITING HIGHLIGHTS
THE WHITE TOWER

This houses part of the Royal Armouries' collection of British arms and armour – some of which are as old as the tower itself. Here you can see a set of armour worn by Henry VIII plus numerous interesting firearms, weapons and military hardware. On the second floor is the Chapel of St John built in the 11th century. It is one of the earliest and finest Romanesque church interiors to survive intact, moving in its simplicity.

TRAITORS' GATE

Traitors' Gate was first called the Water Gate, but the name was later changed when it was used as the landing for the Crown's enemies. All important prisoners entered the Tower here. It is reported that when Princess Elizabeth was imprisoned by her half-sister Mary Tudor, arriving on Palm Sunday 1554, she refused at first to land at the gate, angrily proclaiming that she was no traitor. A sharp

THE RAVENS

There are always at least six ravens kept next to the Wakefield Tower at the government's expense. They are tended by one of the Yeoman Warders who is known as the Ravenmaster. An ancient legend states that if they leave the Tower, it, and the whole kingdom, will crumble. Ravens can live on average up to the age of 25 but some have been known to reach 45 years. The ravens have their wings clipped on one side to prevent them flying away from the Tower.

The view of Traitor's Gate from inside the tower.

shower of rain however, caused her to change her mind. Later when she visited the Tower as queen she insisted on passing through Traitors' Gate. 'What was good enough for Elizabeth the Princess is good enough for Elizabeth the Queen,' she is supposed to have told the Constable.

CHAPEL ROYAL OF ST PETER AD VINCULA

The original church of St Peter's existed before the Tower and was incorporated into its structure. It takes its name 'St Peter in chains' from the miracle in which an angel was said to have set Peter free when imprisoned by King Herod. It has been rebuilt many times over the centuries – the existing structure dates from Tudor times.

The chapel has many beautiful monuments and effigies and a 17th-century organ carved by Grinling Gibbons. It is the parish church of the Tower and the burial place of many of those executed there, including Anne Boleyn, Catherine Howard, Lady Jane Grey, Thomas More and John Fisher.

SCAFFOLD GREEN

Just by the Chapel of St Peter ad Vincula lies the small square of green where so many lost their lives. It is now marked by a striking circular glass memorial by the artist Brian Catling (see opposite).

Anne Boleyn, the second wife of Henry VIII, was dispatched by a skilled swordsman from Calais in 1536 after being found guilty of incest and adultery.

> *'I heard say that the executioner was very good, and I have a little neck.'*
> **Anne Boleyn before her execution, to the Constable of the Tower.**

In 1541 Margaret, Countess of Salisbury whose main offence was being the last surviving member of the Plantagenets, was executed at the age of 67. Henry VIII's fourth wife, Catherine Howard, aged only 19, was killed with a single axe blow after a trial found her guilty of committing adultery and Viscountess Rochford who had acted as

a go-between was also executed. The night before her death Catherine practised laying her head on the block.

The body was buried in an unmarked grave in St Peter's ad Vincula and when Queen Victoria had the chapel restored, Catherine's remains were identified. She is now commemorated on the plaque on the chapel's West Wall along with others who died on the Tower Green scaffold. Catherine's two lovers were not so fortunate and were first tortured in the Tower then publicly executed at Tyburn and their heads displayed on pikes on London Bridge.

The nine-day queen, Lady Jane Grey, was beheaded in 1554 and finally Robert Devereaux, the Earl of Essex, once Queen Elizabeth I's favourite, mounted the Tower Green scaffold.

> *'Here lie before the high altar two dukes between two queens, to wit, the Duke of Somerset and the Duke of Northumberland, between Queen Anne and Queen Kathrine, all four beheaded'* John Stow, Historian 1525–1605

BLOODY TOWER

This dates from the reigns of Edward III and Richard II and was so called as early as 1597, being believed to be the scene of the murder of the two princes: Edward V and his brother, the Duke of York (see pages 85-6). It was originally known as the Garden Tower, as it faced an open space which was formerly the Constable of the Tower's garden. Sir Walter Raleigh spent many years immured here.

THE WAKEFIELD TOWER

Here there are exhibits of medieval and later instruments of torture including the rack. Guy Fawkes suffered ten days of questioning and was doubtless stretched on such a device to make him confess in November 1605. It was last used in 1640.

BEAUCHAMP TOWER

Its name probably refers to the imprisonment there of Thomas Beauchamp, third Earl of Warwick, who was attainted in 1397, during the reign of Richard II,

A Beefeater or Yeoman Warder to give him his official title.

but restored to his honours and liberty two years later by Henry IV. Many others were imprisoned there and the interior walls are still covered with fascinating graffiti and inscriptions carved by prisoners.

THE CROWN JEWELS

This unique collection is housed in the Jewel House which was opened in 1994. It is one of the finest in the world and includes not only the regalia used at coronations, but also crowns acquired by various monarchs, a mass of gold banqueting and church plate, orders, insignia, robes and a unique collection of medals and royal christening fonts.

The Crown Jewels include the Imperial State Crown which is still used at coronations and at the State Opening of Parliament. It is set with 2,836 diamonds, 273 pearls, 17 sapphires, 11 emeralds and 5 rubies and weighs over 2.5 pounds. It incorporates many famous jewels including a large ruby worn by the Black Prince, a beautifully coloured blue sapphire from Edward the Confessor's ring, large egg-shaped pearls that were once earrings worn by Queen Elizabeth I and the incredible Cullinan diamond.

HISTORY OF THE CROWN JEWELS

The Crown Jewels have been kept at the Tower of London since 1303 after they were stolen from Westminster Abbey. It is thought that most of the pieces, if not all, were recovered shortly afterwards.

In 1649, after the Civil War and the execution of Charles I, the new parliamentary government dispersed and sold most of the jewels and regalia both to raise money and because they were symbolic of the 'detestable rule of kings'. Replacements for the lost regalia were made for Charles II's coronation in 1661 and today the collection of crowns and jewels is one of the finest in the world.

After the coronation of Charles II, they were locked away and could only be seen on payment of a fee paid to the custodian. However, this arrangement ended when in 1671 Colonel Thomas Blood attempted to steal the Crown Jewels after having bound and gagged the custodian. Thereafter, the Crown Jewels were kept in a part of the Tower known as the Jewel House, where armed guards defended them. They were temporarily taken out of the Tower in the Second World War and moved to a secret hiding place.

WHERE TO STAY

GENERAL INFORMATION

The British Hotel Reservation centre (BHRC) has information desks at Heathrow and Gatwick airports and at Victoria train and coach stations. There is no charge for booking a room through them and they are open daily from 6.00 am until midnight.
020 7828 0601; www.bhrc.co.uk.

Thomas Cook charges a nominal fee of £5 to book rooms and has desks at Gatwick Airport and the British Visitor Centre on Lower Regent Street. 01293 529372

Online booking is possible at www.londontown.com. A fee is paid to the hotel when you check out.

It is obviously best to consult a reputable guidebook for a full listing of hotels and B & Bs in London but a sample are listed below:

NORTH LONDON

78 Albert Street B & B (near Camden Town tube, Regent's Park and Zoo)
020 7387 6813 joanna@peterbellarchitects.com

La Gaffe Hotel (Hampstead Village, Hampstead Underground)
020 7435 4941 www.lagaffe.co.uk

MARYLEBONE / BAKER STREET

La Place Hotel (near Baker Street tube) 020 7486 2323 www.hotellaplace.com

Wigmore Court B & B (Marble Arch tube) 020 7935 0928 www.wigmore-court-hotel.co.uk

BLOOMSBURY

Russell Hotel (Russell Square tube) 020 7837 6470 www.lemeridien.com

Crescent B &B (Russell Square or Euston tube) 020 7389 1515

CENTRAL

Hazlitt's (Tottenham Court Road tube) 020 7434 1771 www.hazlittshotel.com

The Fielding (Covent Garden tube) 020 7836 8305 www.the-fielding-hotel.co.uk

NOTTING HILL / KENSINGTON

26 Hillgate Place B & B (Notting Hill tube) 020 7727 7717 www. 26hillgateplace.co.uk

The Gore Hotel (South Kensington or High Street Kensington tube)
020 7584 6601 www.gorehotel.co.uk

VICTORIA

Tophams Hotel (Victoria tube or mainline station) 020 7730 8147 www.tophams.co.uk

Oxford House B & B (Victoria tube or mainline station) 020 7834 6467

SOUTH OF THE RIVER

The Bowling Hall B & B (Oval or Kennington tube)
020 7840 0454 email bowlinghall@freenet.co.uk

London County Hall Travel Inn (Waterloo or Westminster tube)
020 7902 1619 www.travelinn.co.uk

108 Streathbourne Road (Tooting Bec tube) 020 8767 6931 www.streathbourneroad.com

Why is this a World Heritage Site?

The whole site is a 'veritable museum of the history of the United Kingdom'. All the buildings are associated with the history of the oldest parliamentary monarchy. Westminster Abbey is a place where kings and queens have been crowned since 1066 and in the Middle Ages the House of Commons used to meet in its chapter house or its refectory. St Margaret's church is known as 'the parish church of the House of Commons'.

Westminster Palace comprises the House of Lords, the House of Commons, the Victoria Tower, the Clock Tower (Big Ben), all constructed in the 19th century around some precious vestiges from medieval times – Westminster Hall, the chapel of St Mary of the Crypt and the Jewel Tower. The complex 'illustrates in colossal proportions, the grandeur of the constitutional monarchy and the principle of the bicameral system.'

The Neo-Gothic architecture of the Parliament buildings echoes the original English Gothic style of Westminster Abbey making the whole area an unbroken ensemble of immense artistic importance.

Location

All buildings are in the City of Westminster on the north side of the Thames. Big Ben abuts Westminster Bridge and the Palace faces the river on one side and Parliament Square on the other. Westminster Abbey, St Margaret's and the Jewel Tower are located on the south side of the square.

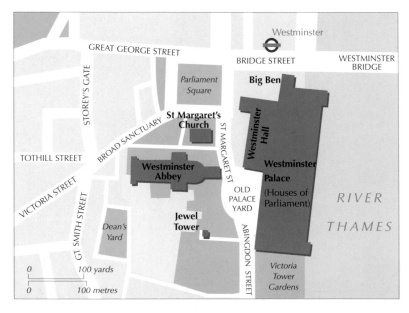

HISTORY AND ARCHITECTURE

Westminster Abbey

In the 1040s King Edward the Confessor re-endowed a Benedictine monastery founded in about 960 situated on Thorney Island by the banks of the River Thames. A large church was built and dedicated to St Peter the Apostle. It was identified as the 'west minster' to differentiate it from St Paul's Cathedral which was known as the 'east minster'.

Today the only remains of this Norman abbey to be seen are in the round arches and columns of the Undercroft. William the Conqueror was crowned in the abbey on Christmas Day 1066 and set the custom for every English monarch with the exception of Edward V and Lady Jane Grey who were deposed before they could be crowned, and Edward VIII who abdicated before his coronation. Henry III was first crowned at Gloucester Abbey (later the Cathedral) as a child before his second coronation at the abbey.

It was Henry III who modelled himself on the pious Edward the Confessor who was responsible for creating the abbey as we see it today. Work began in 1245 during the golden age of Gothic architecture – when the cathedrals of Amiens and Chartres were built in France and Winchester and Salisbury in England. Westminster Abbey is probably the English Gothic church which displays the heaviest French influence in its proportions and plan: it has the highest interior height of 32 metres (103 ft) of any English Gothic church.

The use of piers of Purbeck marble with their dark colours of grey, green and purple is one of the Abbey's special characteristics. In 1269 the Abbey was consecrated and the remains of Edward the Confessor – who had been sanctified as St Edward – were moved to a new shrine.

Another royal burial in 1422 occasioned a change in the Abbey. Henry V, victor of Agincourt, was laid to rest at the eastern end of St Edward's Chapel and in accordance with his will a chantry chapel was constructed over the tomb with two turreted staircases leading to an altar above.

Between 1503 and 1519 the first Tudor king, Henry VII, began a new Lady Chapel which has been described

The west front of Westminster Abbey. The towers, designed by Nicholas Hawksmoor, were completed in 1745.

THE CORONATION CHAIR AND THE STONE OF SCONE

This oak chair was made by Master Walter, the King's Painter in 1300–1. It was designed specifically to hold the Stone of Scone in its base. This had been seized from Scotland – where it was known as the 'Stone of Destiny' and had been used for ancient Scottish coronations – by Edward I in 1296 together with other important Scottish icons of nationhood. (Edward is famously described on his tomb in Westminster Abbey as the 'Hammer of the Scots'.) In 1996 the Stone was finally returned to Edinburgh and is now displayed in Edinburgh Castle until the next coronation when its temporary return to England has been promised. Westminster schoolboys and visitors have over the years damaged the back of the chair by carving their names in it. Four lions were added to the base of the chair in Tudor times although the present ones are 18th-century replacements.

as Late Perpendicular Gothic style 'at its best, both sturdy and sumptuous'. Its walls are decorated with more than 100 figures of superb quality but its greatest attraction is the fan vaulted roof which is enchanting and spectacular.

The final chapter in the Abbey's construction was in the 18th century when the West Towers were completed to a design by Nicholas Hawksmoor.

Unlike most of England's monastic buildings the Abbey survived destruction during Henry VIII's Dissolution of the Monasteries because of its unique relationship with the monarchy and parliament as coronation and burial church for England's kings and queens. Today it is neither a cathedral nor a parish church but a 'Royal Peculiar' under the jurisdiction of the Dean and Chapter, subject only to the sovereign.

MONUMENTS

Westminster Abbey is the home of more than 600 monuments and statues and to be thus honoured is one of the highest accolades that British society can bestow on an individual. To some the plethora of memorials has disfigured the interior. Pugin spoke of 'the incongruous and detestable monuments' and William Morris characterised them as 'the most hideous specimens of false art that can be found in the whole world'. Only a visitor can decide if their sheer exuberance and variety, plus their historical associations, overcome these objections.

Apart from the 28 kings and queens who are buried here, there are memorials to a diverse range of people from poets such as William Blake and Robert Browning, to the great engineers Richard Trevithick and Isambard Kingdom Brunel, the philosopher and scientist Isaac Newton, the musician George Frederic Handel, the astronomers William Herschel and Jeremiah Horrox and great reformers from William Wilberforce to Martin Luther King. The list is huge and, of course, apart from those memorialised there are over three thousand people actually buried in the church and its cloisters.

St Margaret's Church

St Margaret's is known as the parish church of the House of Commons and is situated between Westminster Abbey and the Houses of Parliament – the ideal companion to the grandeur of the Abbey. One is steeped in royal associations, the other reflecting the power of Parliament.

HISTORY AND ARCHITECTURE

The original monks of Westminster Abbey built this church so that local people could attend it without disturbing them at their own devotions. The church is dedicated to the 4th-century saint, St Margaret of Antioch. Although it was originally built in the late 11th century there were many later additions and restorations and it was largely reconstructed in the 15th century as it had fallen into disrepair.

Its style is Late Perpendicular and like Westminster Abbey it contains many splendid monuments but they are not out of proportion with the whole. The stained glass in the East window may have been created in the Netherlands to celebrate the wedding of Katherine of Aragon and Henry VIII in 1509. Other windows commemorate William Caxton (who established Britain's first printing press), buried in the church in 1491, Sir Walter Raleigh, executed in Old Palace Yard and then buried in the church in 1618, and the poet John Milton, a parishioner of the church. Look out for the John Piper window of 1966, notable for its abstract style and colour.

CONNECTIONS WITH THE HOUSE OF COMMONS

Many MPs use the church for weddings, baptisms and other services, following in the footsteps of Samuel Pepys and Winston Churchill both of whom were married here. In 1614, during what is known as the 'Addled Parliament', the whole House of Commons took Holy Communion together in the church on Palm Sunday, 17 April: they preferred the simple services of St Margaret's. This Parliament refused to grant James I money from taxation until their grievances were settled. The king dissolved Parliament and did not call another one until 1621.

In 1681 a pew was set aside for the Speaker of the House of Commons. It is on the south side of the church and has the crowned portcullis emblem of Parliament carved on the pew end. The portcullis symbol is found everywhere in the church – on hassocks, curtains and doors.

HISTORY AND ARCHITECTURE

Palace of Westminster

The palace became the main residence of the kings and queens of England from the reign of Edward the Confessor in the 11th century until that of Henry VIII in the 16th. Westminster Hall, the oldest surviving part of the medieval palace, was built by William Rufus, the son of William the Conqueror; it was the largest Norman hall in England. All the administrative, judicial and parliamentary business of the court was carried out in the palace.

By 1332 the Lords and Commons met separately and, although the Lords met in the palace itself, the Commons had no fixed place to gather and therefore went to the octagonal chapter house or the now destroyed refectory of Westminster Abbey. By 1363 the Commons had its own clerk, and by 1377 a Speaker, who was designated to speak to the monarch on the behalf of the Commons. In 1547 when private chapels were abolished under the Chantry Act, the Commons was granted the use of the royal chapel of St Stephen's within the confines of the palace as their

The Palace of Westminster from Westminster Bridge.

meeting place. In 1707 Sir Christopher Wren was employed to alter and enlarge the ancient chapel but his efforts only succeeded in reducing one of the glories of medieval architecture to a drab and uncomfortable space. The chamber became very overcrowded over the centuries as two Acts of Union, first with Scotland in 1707, and then with Ireland in 1801, added to the number of members of the Commons.

In October 1834 a fire destroyed both Houses of Lords and Commons. *The Times* wrote 'the spectacle was one of surpassing though terrific splendour. The conflagration viewed from the river, was peculiarly grand and impressive.' In a huge effort Westminster Hall was saved and luckily the Jewel Tower where many historical documents were stored did not catch fire.

Temporary accommodation was ready for the resumption of parliamentary business within three months and a competition was announced for architects to submit designs for a new palace. It was decided after furious argument that the architectural style of the new building should be in either the Elizabethan or Gothic form. It became in the words of the UNESCO recommendation, 'an outstanding, coherent and complete example of Neo-Gothic style'.

From 97 entries the winning submission was that of Charles Barry (1795–1860). One of the reasons he won was as a result of the 'minute drawings' which

ST STEPHEN'S CHAPEL

The lay-out of the chapel consisted of steep rows of choir stalls which faced each other across an aisle. At the west end there was a screen with double doors at its centre. When the Commons first occupied the chapel in 1547 they adapted to their new surroundings and sat opposite one another across the aisle. Previously they had sat in a circle in the Abbey Chapter House, but now the seating arrangements in their new home gradually contributed to a sharper political differentiation.

They used the right-hand side of the door in the screen for the 'Ayes' votes and the left for the 'Noes'. The Speaker in the modern House of Commons still orders 'Ayes to the right, Noes to the left' when Members of Parliament vote in a division.

In the 17th century they put green serge over the hard wooden pews and green is still the colour of the House seats today.

were the work of his brilliant assistant Augustus Pugin (1812–52). Both Barry and Pugin believed that every internal and external surface of the building should be decorated. The triumph of the final buildings was the result of the fruitful collaboration between these two men with their different talents and personalities – the reliable Barry who was able to deal with the numerous committees and commissions overseeing the work and the hyperactive Pugin whom Barry described as 'his comet'.

The Sovereign's Entrance in the Victoria Tower.

FACTS AND FIGURES

The site covers 3.3 hectares (8 acres) of land and originally needed 21,000 cubic metres (740,000 cubic ft) of stone to build a palace of 1,180 rooms, 126 staircases, more than 2 miles of corridors, 15 miles of steam pipes with 1,200 stopcocks. It was the largest single building ever undertaken in Great Britain at that time. Before work began the Thames had to be dammed and a raft of concrete laid to stabilise the ground. An army of masons, builders, craftsmen and artists worked for over 50 years to complete the project.

THE CENTRAL LOBBY

The Central Lobby – originally called the Central Hall – is the focal point of the Palace. It is an impressive octagon with four large doorways and four diagonal windows and this is where members of the public wait to see their MPs. The brass chandelier weighs three tons and can be raised and lowered by an electric motor. From the Lobby, corridors leads northwards to the House of Commons Lobby and Chamber and south to the House of Lords.

THE QUEEN'S ROBING ROOM AND ROYAL GALLERY

Beyond the House of Lords are the splendid ceremonial rooms used for the State Opening of Parliament, and the Royal Gallery. In the Robing Room the decorative skills of Pugin are seen at their best – not an inch of space is without pattern and colour. The frescoes on the wall are by William Dyce and represent Hospitality, Mercy, Courtesy, Religion and Generosity, based on the legend of King Arthur.

The monarch passes through the Royal Gallery on her way to the House of Lords. It is decorated by Daniel Maclise with two huge paintings: 'The Death of Nelson at the Battle of Trafalgar' and 'The Battle of Waterloo'.

The Victoria Tower.

House of Lords

The 19th-century writer Nathaniel Hawthorne said of the House of Lords: 'Nothing could be more magnificent and gravely gorgeous.' The colours of rich brown and gold are a perfect foil to the red leather seats and woolsack. The grand throne with its canopy and flanking candelabra is magnificent and the entire Chamber is an elaborate recreation of heraldic designs and coats of arms.

House of Commons

The original Victorian Lobby of the House of Commons and the Chamber itself were destroyed during the Second World War as a result of German bombing. It was rebuilt by Sir Giles Gilbert Scott in the same style as the original Gothic but some of the rich details of ornamentation were lost. However, all the old traditions remain such as the original Mace which must rest on the central table when the House is sitting. The Mace is a symbol of royal authority and without its presence the House is considered powerless. The government benches are on the right of the Speaker with the opposition to his left; the lay-out echoes that of the old chapel that the Commons once occupied (see Fact Box page 98).

The Three Towers

The vast area of the Palace is broken up by the asymmetrical arrangement of three towers and the exterior frontages ripple with the flourishes of Pugin's carved figures, crockets and finials.

The Victoria Tower

This tower is just over 100 metres high (336 ft) and features the sovereign's entrance at its base. It was intended as a place to keep state documents and still fulfils this function. The tower took on the role of a Norman keep and on State Openings soldiers are stationed in the turrets overlooking Whitehall. As the royal procession comes into view they signal to the Royal Horse Artillery in Hyde Park to fire the Royal Salute just as the State Coach arrives at its destination.

Clock Tower – Big Ben

At the north-eastern end of the Palace is the Clock Tower which houses the world's largest four-faced, chiming turret clock known by all as 'Big Ben'. The name actually refers to the main bell which weighs over 13 tons thought by some to be named after the commissioner of works, Sir Benjamin Hall, but by others after a popular heavyweight boxer of the time, Benjamin Caunt. The architectural historian, Nikolaus Pevsner's view is that it has a 'completely unorthodox top, a fairy tower of no archaeological precedent' and has become a symbol of London all over the world. The tower is 96 metres high (315 ft); the first 61 metres (200 ft), the Clock Tower, is constructed in brickwork with stone cladding, the remainder being a framed spire of cast iron. See below for details of how to visit the Clock Tower.

How the Clock Tower was built

The tower was built entirely from the inside outwards with no exterior scaffolding. A wooden platform inside the tower was fitted with rails and a mobile crane moved around the rails bringing up building materials from below. As the building grew the platform was slowly raised by six giant screws. It was a superb piece of Victorian engineering and inventiveness.

The Central Tower

Like an elegant church steeple the Central Tower rises above the roofscape. It was not in the original plans but was included to ensure sufficient ventilation and although it was never needed for that purpose it is a graceful addition to the whole design.

Westminster Hall

Over a thousand years old, this Norman hall has survived the perils of the great fire of 1834, German bombs and deathwatch beetle. The original walls were built by William Rufus in 1097–99 and the Hall is the oldest extant structure on the Palace of Westminster site. It is 73 metres in length (240 ft) and was used for

Gunpowder Plot

The conspiracy to detonate a huge stock of gunpowder beneath the Houses of Parliament during the the ceremonial opening of Parliament by James I on 5 November 1605 has become a key date in the collective memory of the British people and the foiling of the plot is still celebrated with fireworks and bonfires throughout the land.

The plan was hatched by a number of fanatical Roman Catholic gentlemen led by Robert Catesby. In May 1604 the group hired a house which abutted the House of Lords. They then tunnelled from the cellars of this dwelling through the shared foundations of the two buildings and secreted 36 barrels of gunpowder beneath the House of Lords. However, the plot was discovered as a result of an anonymous letter to a Catholic peer warning him not to attend on 5 November. A thorough search on 4 November revealed one of the conspirators, Guy Fawkes, who under extreme torture divulged the names of the members of the group who were quickly rounded up and subsequently executed.

The discovery of the plot deepened general hatred of British Catholics who became the subject of discriminatory and penal laws.

Visitor Information

Palace of Westminster

Please see www.parliament.uk for up-to-date information including security points regarding access.

Access to the Houses of Parliament

Visitors who tour Parliament will see the key areas such as the Commons and Lords debating chambers and the Queen's Robing Room. UK residents can tour throughout the year; overseas visitors may only tour during the Summer Opening. Accompanied by a trained guide, visitors travel through designated areas of the parliamentary estate. Tours take about 75 minutes.

UK residents only

Free tours are held throughout the year, and you need to arrange a place through your MP or a member of the House of Lords. Overseas visitors pay for a tour during the Summer Opening, in advance or by queuing on the day.

UK and overseas visitors

During the Summer Opening, UK residents and overseas visitors can buy tickets to tour Parliament. These tours are arranged during the summer recess, when Parliament does not sit. Tours run from Monday to Saturday inclusive, but not on Sunday or Bank Holidays. Tours take about 75 minutes. Opening is usually from 31 July to 29 September. The route visitors take through Parliament during the Summer Opening is identical to the tours run during session. UK residents may organise a free tour through their MP while the Summer Opening is happening, but times are restricted to certain mornings, due to the extra volume of visitors.

Tickets

Tickets are available on the day from the Ticket Office located next to the Jewel Tower in Old Palace Yard (opposite the Houses of Parliament). Visitors are advised to pre-book tours in advance by calling 0870 906 3773. Under fives go free but still require a ticket for entrance – however, please note that tours are not recommended for young children as there is a lot of walking. Pushchairs are allowed, but larger models will not fit in certain areas.

Tour times

August: Monday, Tuesday, Friday, Saturday: 9.15 am – 4.30 pm
Wednesday, Thursday: 1.15 – 4.30 pm

September: Monday, Friday, Saturday: 9.15 am – 4.30 pm
Tuesday, Wednesday, Thursday: 1.15 – 4.30 pm

Foreign languages

There are foreign language tours at set times in French, Spanish, Italian and German. If a group of visitors book out an entire tour time then an interpreter for any language may be brought along by the group.

Bags

Bags or luggage larger than those permitted in aircraft cabins may be refused entry. Parliament has no facilities for leaving items; commercial outlets are available nearby at Victoria and Charing Cross stations.

Visiting the Clock Tower

It is possible to visit the Clock Tower and tours are free and open to UK residents who have requested a visit through their local MP. Children under the age of 11 are not permitted. When demand is high those with a proven interest in clocks or bells will be given preference. Visitors to the Clock Tower will be shown up by a guide, who will outline the history of the tower, the bell and how the most accurate public clock in the world works.

Tours for overseas visitors are currently not permitted.

Central England

Blenheim Palace

Derwent Valley Mills

Ironbridge Gorge

Liverpool
Sheffield

CHESHIRE
Chester

DERBYSHIRE

Stoke on Trent

NOTTS

Derwent Valley Mills

Nottingham

Derby

Ironbridge Gorge
Shrewsbury

STAFFORDSHIRE

LEICESTERSHIRE

SALOP

WEST

Leicester

Birmingham

MIDLANDS

HEREFORD
AND
WORCESTER

WARWICK
SHIRE
NORTHANTS

Hereford

WALES
Gloucester

Blenheim Palace

GLOUCESTERSHIRE
Oxford

Cardiff

OXFORDSHIRE

Bristol

0   25 miles
0   40 kms

Blenheim Palace

A Triumph of the Baroque set in a Princely Park

Date of Inscription 1986

Why is it a World Heritage Site?

Blenheim is a rare example of a European 18th-century building of the type that would normally be built for a monarch – such as Versailles. More of a national monument than just a stately home its unique architecture draws on Elizabethan, French and Italian influences and was to prove influential in Britain and elsewhere. Moreover the whole setting of the palace within the park, laid out by 'Capability' Brown, was part of, and an inspiration for, the English Romantic movement.

The Palace was a gift to John Churchill, Duke of Marlborough by Queen Anne, in gratitude for his military victories over the French in the War of the Spanish Succession. The name of Blenheim is an anglicised version of Blindheim in Bavaria, the site of his most famous victory, in 1704.

Location

Blenheim Palace and its park are near the town of Woodstock in Oxfordshire, approximately 8 miles (12 kms) north west of Oxford.

HISTORY AND ARCHITECTURE

Queen Anne's gift included the Royal Manor of Woodstock and funds of £240,000 for the construction of the palace. A first sight of the golden stones of Blenheim with its grand portico, its columns, colonnades, multiple towers, turrets and pinnacles shows how superlatively the architect Sir John Vanbrugh fulfilled his aim of creating a truly impressive edifice and why King George III made his

remarkable observation while on a visit in 1786, 'We have nothing to equal this!'

The size and splendour of Blenheim Palace dwarfs other British royal palaces and indeed it was criticised for this as early as 1712 by Lord Shaftesbury as 'a false and counterfeit piece of magnificence, as can justly be arraign'd for its Deformity.'

John Vanbrugh was a surprising choice as an architect as his main claim to fame were his comic plays such as *The Provok'd Wife*, but his plans for Castle Howard in Yorkshire had impressed the duke. Vanbrugh was to collaborate with the more experienced Nicholas Hawksmoor on the building and Christopher Wren was also consulted. During the course of its construction the combative Duchess of Marlborough (described as 'at warfare with the whole world') fell out of favour with Queen Anne and funds for the building dried up. The Marlboroughs went into exile and returned only after the queen died. They then finished the palace at their own expense but shortly afterwards the quarrelsome duchess fell out with Vanbrugh and the supervision of the project was taken over by a cabinetmaker, John Moore.

'When the Queen declared she would build a house in Woodstock Park for the Duke of Marlborough and that she meant it in memory of the great services he had done her and the nation, I found it... ought... to be considered both as a Royall and a National Monument and care taken in the design, and the execution, that it might have the qualitys proper to such a monument, viz, Beauty, Magnificence and Duration...'

John Vanbrugh, architect

The style of Blenheim defies a narrow classification and although the word 'Baroque' is often used, Vanbrugh's conception has many roots – notably his interest in medieval fortresses and castles. The fantastical skyline is reminiscent of Elizabethan houses and there are also echoes of Versailles as well as Italian influences. In reality it is a unique design that did not follow the prevailing fashion of French classicism but was in some respects a precursor of English Romanticism.

VISITING THE PALACE
THE EAST GATE AND CLOCK TOWER
This bears an inscription setting out how the palace came to be built. The first courtyard then leads to the great Clock Tower decorated with two huge lions, carved by Grinling Gibbons, clasping the cockerel of France in their paws. This leads to the Great Court where at last one can see the main entrance.

THE GREAT HALL
The main entrance leads straight into a 20 metre (65 ft) high Great Hall with two tiers of stone arches on either side. Grinling Gibbons carved the cornices and the Corinithian capitals. The magnificent painted ceiling is by Sir James

DUKE OF MARLBOROUGH (1650-1722)

John Churchill was bought up in straitened circumstances in Devon as a result of his father, Winston Churchill's support for Charles I in the Civil War. However, the Restoration of Charles II brought a change of fortune for John's father who was given a post at court and a knighthood. John's sister, Arabella, became the mistress of James, Duke of York and John himself became a page to the duke. He gained a commission in the guards in 1667 and in 1678 he was appointed a colonel in the British army.

When James became king in 1685, Churchill played a major role in crushing the Duke of Monmouth's rebellion; but just three years later, Churchill abandoned the Catholic king James for the Protestant William of Orange.

Honoured at William's coronation, Churchill, now the Earl of Marlborough, served with distinction in Ireland and Flanders during the War of the Grand Alliance. However, the relationship between Marlborough and the dual monarchs William and Mary remained cool. After damaging allegations of collusion with the exiled court of King James, Marlborough was dismissed from all civil and military offices and temporarily imprisoned in the Tower of London. Only after the death of Mary, and the threat of another major European war, did Marlborough return to favour with William.

Marlborough's influence at court reached its zenith with the accession of his wife Sarah's close friend Queen Anne. Promoted to Captain-General of British forces, and later to a dukedom, Marlborough found international fame in the War of the Spanish Succession where, on the fields of Blenheim (1704), Ramillies (1706), Oudenarde (1708) and Malplaquet (1709) his place in history as one of Europe's great generals (and perhaps Britain's greatest) was assured. Always popular with his men Marlborough led by the example of his own personal courage.

However, when his wife fell from royal grace as Queen Anne's favourite, the Tories, determined on peace with France, pressed for his downfall. Marlborough was dismissed again from all offices on charges of embezzlement, but the duke eventually regained favour with the accession of George I in 1714. Although returned to his former offices, the duke's health soon deteriorated and, after a series of strokes, he eventually died on 27 June 1722.

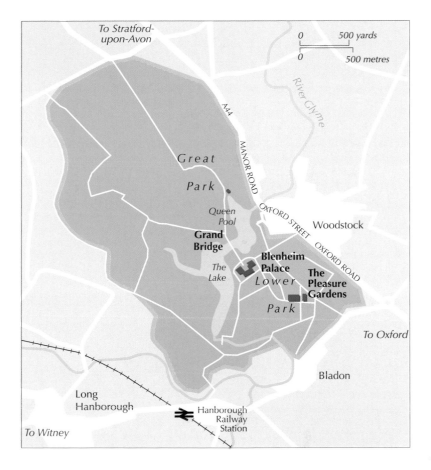

Thornhill and shows the first duke kneeling in front of Britannia presenting his battle plan for Blenheim.

By taking a corridor to the right of the hall you will arrive at the small bedroom where Winston Churchill was born on 30 November 1874 to Lady Randolph Churchill. There is also an exhibition looking at Winston Churchill's life and achievements. Churchill proposed to his wife in the Temple of Diana in the grounds and was a frequent visitor to the palace throughout his life (see box).

CHINA ANTEROOM
In the China anteroom are displays of Meissen and Sèvres porcelain. The Meissen service with its sliced lemon handles was presented to the 3rd Duke by the King of Poland in exchange for a pack of staghounds.

GREEN AND RED DRAWINGS ROOMS
The grand Green and Red drawing rooms are a showcase for numerous portraits and rococo mirrors. The ceilings are the work of Hawksmoor and their banding and coving lend richness to these elegant rooms.

Winston Churchill (1874–1965)

'At Blenheim I took two very important decisions: to be born and marry'

Churchill was born in a small bedroom near to the Great Hall. His mother Lady Randolph Churchill (Jennie Jerome) had been a celebrated American society beauty before her marriage. He was two months premature and it seems that this room was chosen in a hurry as it was part of the chaplain's apartments. After school at Harrow he attended the military academy of Sandhurst and began his army career in India.

In 1900 he entered Parliament. During August 1908 he proposed to his great love Clementine Hozier in the Temple of Diana in the grounds of Blenheim. There is a plaque commemorating the event. They then spent part of their honeymoon at Blenheim and were frequent visitors to the palace.

Winston Churchill held many important cabinet posts over the years. He started his parliamentary life as a Conservative but in 1908, at the age of 33, he entered the cabinet as President of the Board of Trade in the Liberal government led by Herbert Asquith. Two years later he was Home Secretary, and in 1911 he became 1st Lord of the Admiralty. During the First World War, his plans to remove Turkey from the war by making an amphibious landing on the Gallipoli peninsula led to disaster and his influence waned. For a while he commanded a battalion on the Western Front. Further cabinet posts in the Liberal government followed but he was defeated in the 1922 general election. In 1924 he returned to government as Chancellor of the Exchequer but this time as a Conservative. His actions during the 1926 General Strike led to the enduring hostility of the working class. With the fall of the Conservative government in 1929, Churchill remained out of office for over ten years.

When at last he was appointed Prime Minister in the perilous early months of 1940 he became an inspirational war leader. After his second spell as Prime Minister in 1951–5 he concentrated on his historical writing. His death in 1965 was marked by a state funeral and he is buried at his own request in the family plot at St Martin's Church in Bladon, near to Woodstock, and in sight of his birthplace at Blenheim.

The Green Writing Room

The beginning of the sequence of the famous Blenheim tapestries can be seen here. Designs were made by the Brussels' weaver Judocus de Vos in the great Flemish tradition. They illustrate in wonderful detail Marlborough's victories and campaigns. The walls are covered in green silk damask recently renewed by the present duke and features his coat of arms.

The Saloon

The ceiling and the *trompe d'oeil* murals are painted by Louis Laguerre and show figures from four continents looking down into the room. On the ceiling is a wildly romantic painting of the Apotheosis of the first duke.

The dining table is used only once a year by the family, on Christmas Day. The silver centrepiece model on the side table is by Garrard and shows Marlborough on horseback after his famous victory writing his dispatch – a copy of which is now in the First State Room.

Over the doors are the armorial bearings of the 1st duke which feature a black, double-headed eagle, the crest of the Holy Roman Empire. The duke had been created a prince of the empire.

THE STATE ROOMS

Three ornate state rooms follow on from the saloon and continue the sequence of tapestries which manage to be both meticulous in their accuracy and yet retain their artistry. In the First State Room is a copy of the famous dispatch Marlborough sent to his wife on the back of a tavern bill proclaiming his victory at Blenheim. The original is held at the British Library.

THE LONG LIBRARY

After the magnificent Baroque style of the State Rooms comes the quieter atmosphere of the Long Library which runs the length of the west front. It is 55 metres (180 ft) long and 10 metres (32ft) high. The design is by Sir Nicholas Hawksmoor who took over as architect after Sarah, the first Duchess of Marlborough quarrelled with Vanbrugh. It was originally envisaged as a picture gallery and it is divided into five sections of varied widths and heights.

There is a statue of Queen Anne by John Michael Rysbrack and at the north end of the library is an enormous Willis organ installed in 1902. The library consists of 10,000 books collected by the 9th duke.

THE CHAPEL

The Chapel is dominated by the marble tomb of the 1st duke and duchess and their two sons – although their four daughters are not included. The duke is shown as a Roman general. The cost was £2,200 and it was designed by William Kent and completed by Michael Rysbrack. A statue of Lord Randolph Churchill, the father of Winston Churchill, can be seen on the south wall.

THE GROUNDS AND GREAT PARK

While there may be some debate as to the beauty of the palace and its success as a piece of architecture, no one can fail to appreciate the picturesque grandeur of the grounds. Much of the original park as envisaged by Vanbrugh was later landscaped to appear 'romantically natural' by 'Capability' Brown. In addition, in the early 20th century, the 9th duke together with the French landscape architect, Duchêne, planted the formal Italian garden and the Water Terraces on the west front.

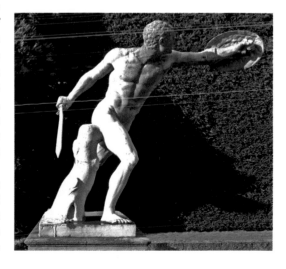

There is also the Secret Garden replanted by the current duke to commemorate the tercentenary of the Battle

A view of the formal gardens at Blenheim.

of Blenheim which is on a more relaxed and intimate scale. The Arboretum with rare trees and incense cedars is especially beautiful in the spring when its banks are covered with yellow daffodils and bluebells. To its right is the Rose Garden planted with scented symmetrical beds of red, pink and white roses.

Beyond the Rose Garden is the Grand Cascade designed by 'Capability' Brown in the mid-18th century. The River Glyme rushes down from the lake and glides under the 'New' Bridge until it joins the River Evenlode. This complements the Grand Bridge by Vanbrugh which was originally built for habitation with up to 30 or more rooms inside it. Building the Grand Bridge involved a lot of heavy engineering work. The ditch between the bridge and the sides of the valley was filled with tons of rubble from the ruins of the old manor at Woodstock. The setting is sublime.

THE COLUMN OF VICTORY
The Column of Victory stands at the entrance to the Great Avenue. It is 40 metres high (134 ft) and is surmounted by a statue by Robert Pit of the 1st duke dressed as a Roman general with eagles at his feet and a Winged Victory in his hand. The monument was completed in 1730 at a cost of £3,000.

OTHER ATTRACTIONS
The Marlborough Maze, the second largest hedge maze in the world, is laid out in pictorial form. Close by there is also a lavender walk, a scale model of Woodstock, putting greens and a giant chess and draughts set plus an adventure play area.

The Butterfly House is home to many tropical butterflies who flutter freely among exotic flowers and hothouse plants. Free-flying Zebra finches complete the experience.

Visitor Information

Opening Times

The Palace, Park and Gardens are open daily from mid-February until the end of October; Wednesdays to Sundays in November and until mid-December. The Park opens at 9.00 am, the Formal Gardens from 10.00 am and the first entry to the Palace is at 10.30 am. When the Palace is closed the Park is open every day (except Christmas Day) from 9.00 am until 4.45 pm.

How to Get there

By Road

Blenheim Palace is close to the historic town of Woodstock. It is 8 miles north west of Oxford on the A44 Evesham road. The Palace is easily accessible from both London and Birmingham and is signposted from Junction 9 of the M40.

By Rail

Trains run regularly from London Paddington to Oxford and vice versa. Call 08457 48 49 50 for up-to-date information or visit www.firstgreatwestern.co.uk or www.chilternrailways.co.uk

By Coach

Coaches run extremely regularly from Victoria Coach station (London) to Gloucester Green (Oxford). A No. 20 bus runs from Gloucester Green to Woodstock.

By Bus

The No. 20 to Woodstock runs from Oxford Train station and Gloucester Green to the gates of Blenheim Palace on Hensington Road in Woodstock. Please ask the bus driver for that stop. The bus runs every 30 minutes.

Places to Stay

Woodstock

Tourist office 01993 813276 www.oxfordshirecotswolds.org

The Bear Hotel 0870 400 8202

The Feathers 01993 812291 www.feathers.co.uk

Manor Farmhouse 01993 812168

Derwent Valley Mills

The Crucible of the Factory System

Date of Inscription 2001

Why is this a World Heritage Site?

The Derwent Valley in rural Derbyshire was crucial to Britain's industrial revolution and the country's subsequent growth. The area was the harbinger of the factory system in Britain which later spread to the wider world. The many surviving 18th and 19th-century industrial mills and canals which cluster around the River Derwent all bear testament to this. The area was also at the forefront of technological changes in the textile industry, many developed by the great pioneer Richard Arkwright.

Location

The site is about 15 miles (23 kms) long and extends from Matlock Bath to Derby along the valley of the River Derwent in central England.

HISTORY

The first milestone in the story of the Derwent Valley was the construction of a Silk Mill in the 1720s in Derby by two brothers, John and Thomas Lombe, which housed three kinds of machinery never before seen in Britain for the manufacture of silk. John Lombe may also have been a pioneer of industrial espionage for it is believed he was poisoned by an Italian woman in revenge for stealing their processes. The mill was five storeys high and was powered by water. The scale of its production and the number of workers employed there were without precedent, marking the beginning of the factory system whereby an unskilled labour force worked a shift system to ensure continuous production.

Half a century later Richard Arkwright built a water-powered spinning mill at Cromford. The work force was large and whole families were used in the process, children being especially useful as they had nimble fingers and could crawl under the machinery. To attract and keep workers was essential and the mill owners built housing, schools and other amenities on site so that a shift system could be adhered to.

'When I consider the striking natural beauties of such a river as the Matlock, and the effect of the seven-storey buildings that have been raised there, and on other beautiful streams, for cotton manufactories, I am inclined to think that nothing can equal them for the purpose of disbeautifying an enchanting piece of scenery...' **Uvedale Price** (***Essays on the Picturesque* 1810**)

The local artist Joseph Wright of Derby was so entranced by the sight of the Cromford cotton mill ablaze with gaslights at night that he painted the scene in 1789. However, many commentators found the new buildings to be a blot on the landscape.

The Derwent Valley sites are remarkable in that so much of this infrastructure has remained intact and can be seen today as a reminder of a glorious industrial past.

MASSON MILLS

This massive redbrick mill in Matlock Bath was built by Richard Arkwright in 1783 and is now a fascinating working textile museum with authentic machinery in place showing how the original mill functioned. It was the only one of Arkwright's mills actually powered by the River Derwent and is a striking building with small lunettes set between Venetian windows. The cupola housed a bell which summoned employees to the mill.

CROMFORD

The village was a small scattered hamlet with defunct lead mines until Richard Arkwright arrived in 1771 and brought dramatic changes. At Cromford he found a constant supply of water from the Bonsall Brook and Cromford Sough which never froze or dried up and he built his first water-powered mill here. He needed unskilled labour as well as weavers and advertised in the *Derby Mercury* for workers. Over the next 20 years he expanded the village and built warehouses, a chapel and houses for his workforce

Sir Richard Arkwright's Masson Mill.

as well as the Greyhound Hotel in the Market Place for important visitors. The Greyhound is a fine house of five bays with a Roman Doric style centre door. In North Street, the terrace housing for his workforce can still be seen with their sash windows and workshops on the top floors. Nearby is the school and school house erected by Arkwright's son in 1832 when laws were passed to ensure that child labourers had to spend at least part of the working day at school.

Also noteworthy in Cromford is the 'Bear Pit' (see left). This is an oval stone-lined pit made in 1785 with a dam and sluice to ensure that the water from Cromford Sough kept the Greyhound Pond full since the pondwater was the main source of power for the mills.

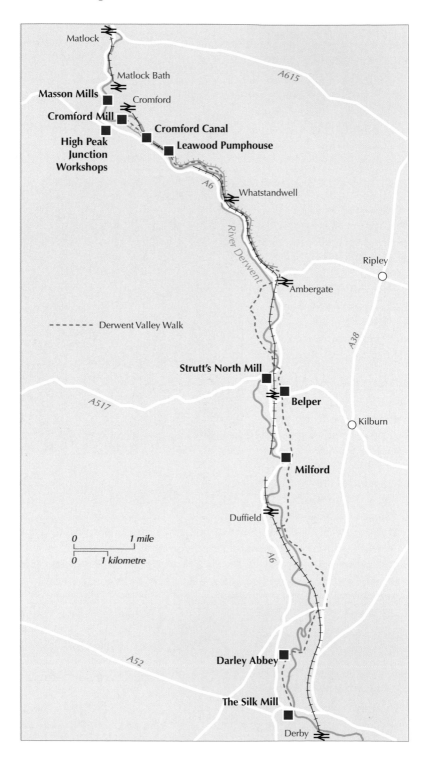

RICHARD ARKWRIGHT (1732-1792)

The jury is still out on Richard Arkwright: was he a forward-looking entrepreneur who found employment for the poor and also helped build Britain's greatness, or a cheat who exploited children and stole other people's ideas?

He was born in Preston, the son of a tailor. The family was too poor to send him to school but a cousin taught him to read and write. He was apprenticed to a barber, becoming a specialist in hair dying and the manufacture of wigs, eventually setting up shop in Bolton. His wigmaking required quantities of human hair and during his travels around the country in pursuit of this commodity he came into contact with weavers and spinners. Arkwright befriended John Kay, a clockmaker from Warrington, who had assisted a certain James Highs in designing a spinning machine which seems to have been the forerunner of Arkwright's spinning frame. However, it was Arkwright who was able to fund the further development of this machine (later known as a Water Frame) which could produce a thread far stronger than anything available at the time and could be used as the warp in the weaving process (unlike the thread produced by Hargreaves' spinning jenny). Equally important to Arkwright, the new machine did not need a skilled person to operate it. So it was Arkwright who took out a patent for the Water Frame in 1775, not those who seem to have been the true inventors, and it was Arkwright who built the mills to exploit this invention and other developments (such as power looms) using steam and water power. In partnership with Derbyshire silk manufacturers Jedediah Strutt and Samuel Need he built a large mill at Cromford and introduced the factory techniques that were to make his fortune. At least two-thirds of his workforce were children from the age of six upwards who worked 13-hour days.

In 1785 the Court of the King's Bench rescinded all his patents but by then Arkwright's fortune was made and he was knighted in 1786.

CROMFORD MILL

This is the earliest industrial building in the Cromford Mill Complex (see right), originally a building of 11 bays and five storeys high using traditional construction of timber beams and sash windows. A fire in 1929 destroyed the two upper storeys and it now houses a permanent exhibition.

CROMFORD CANAL

Constructed in the 1790s it ran 15 miles (23 km) from Cromford, parallel with the Derwent, to join the Erewash Canal as part of a route to Manchester. At Cromford Wharf, warehouses, counting houses and two cottages remain. It is now a place to enjoy a quiet walk and is a haven for wildlife and flowers.

STRUTT'S NORTH MILL, BELPER

This innovatory fireproof mill was built in 1804 by William Strutt. It was the largest cotton factory in England in the early 19th century but business declined when the cotton industry moved to Lancashire.

One of the most technically advanced building of its day, the mill incorporated iron frames with arched hollow pot ceilings. It had a warm air central heating system, a school room in the roof space and a goods lift between floors. It was powered by a great breast-shot water wheel. Each of the five floors housed different stages of the cotton spinning process from the raw cotton bales to the finished thread. There were 68 spinning frames on the first and second floors and 130 carding machines on the third and fourth floors. On the sixth floor in the attic there was a schoolroom where the child employees learnt their 3 'Rs' on Sundays.

BELPER

Belper is situated halfway between Cromford and Derby. Strutt's North Mill lies to the north of the modern town and is overshadowed by the huge East Mill of red Accrington brick which was built in 1912. Five other industrial buildings and mills built by the Strutts were demolished in 1959 and the 1960s. Originally Belper was famous for its nail industry and if your surname is 'Naylor' it is likely that your ancestors originated in Belper. When the Strutts built their mills in the 18th century they also endowed the town with houses for their workforce. The chapel and its nearby cottages were among the first buildings commissioned by Jedediah Strutt who was a Unitarian and a most enlightened employer, concerned for the welfare of his workforce, providing them with schools and establishing his own local farms in order to provide his workers with fresh and wholesome food.

A tour of the town can be arranged at the Visitor Centre in the North Mill.

'SLATER THE TRAITOR' (1768-1835)

Belper is twinned with Pawtucket, Rhode Island. The connection is Samuel Slater of Milford who was an apprentice to Jedediah Strutt but who, having finished his apprenticeship, absconded to the United States disguised as a farm labourer in order to evade laws banning the emigration of those with commercially sensitive knowledge. On arrival in Pawtucket he duly opened his own cotton mill, employing the latest technology learnt whilst with Strutt. This gained him the lasting hatred of his former colleagues in Belper who feared the loss of their jobs as a result of foreign competition and who dubbed him 'Slater the Traitor'. However, to his new countrymen he was nothing less than the father of America's own industrial revolution, President Andrew Jackson calling him the 'Father of American Manufactures'.

MILFORD

The Strutts bought land in Milford in 1781 and built a large complex of cotton mills and bleach works most of which were demolished in the 1960s. However, much of the town itself survives with its industrial terraces and ironwork.

DARLEY ABBEY

This site is within walking distance of Derby's city centre and was founded by Walter Evans in 1783. Five mills were built there of which four remain, constituting the most complete survival of any of the early cotton factory sites in the area. The Long Mill of 1789 was built to replace an earlier building destroyed by fire. The wood inside is sheathed in metal for fire resistance. The East and West Mills were built as later extensions to the 1789 factory.

Many of the houses built by the Evans family for the workforce are also still standing, notably Flat Square, Hill Square, Mile Ash Lane and Brick Row; all of which were connected to one of England's first sewage disposal systems. The church of St Matthew and the school were also erected by the Evans family for the people of the town.

The town's name derives from an old Augustinian priory of which very little survives today. However, the priory buttery still stands and is now the Abbey public house (see below) which serves good beers and excellent pub food.

THE SILK MILL – DERBY'S MUSEUM OF INDUSTRY AND HISTORY

The Silk Mill Museum is on the site of John Lombe's first Silk Mill built by George Sorocold between 1702 and 1717. The foundations and parts of the tower from the 1717 mill are still visible.

Visitor Information

Masson Mills

Open daily except for Christmas Day and Easter Day.
Mon – Fri 10.00 am – 4.00 pm: Saturday 11.00 am – 5.00 pm: Sunday 11.00 am – 4.00 pm.
01629 581001 www.massonmills.co.uk

Cromford Mill

Open daily 9.00 am – 5.00 pm except for Christmas Day.
01629 823256 www.arkwrightsociety.org.uk

Strutt's North Mill

Open Summer (March–October), Wednesday to Sunday and Bank Holiday Mondays
1.00 pm to 5.00 pm.
Other times by arrangement, 01773 880474.
Winter (November– February) Saturday and Sunday 1.00 pm to 5.00 pm.
Closed Christmas Day.

The Silk Mill – Derby

Open daily Monday: 11.00 am – 5.00 pm, Tuesdays – Saturdays 10.00 am – 5.00 pm,
Sundays 1.00 pm – 5.00 pm. 01332 255308.

How to get there

By road

Matlock Bath at the north of the World Heritage Site is on the A6 to the north of Derby.

Public transport

The Derwent Valley Mills World Heritage Site has a good network of bus and rail services,
which provide an alternative to the frustrations of the congested A6 road, particularly
in the summer. Visitors will find there are frequent links from neighbouring towns and
cities.

By rail

Derby is well served by the national rail network with direct services from many parts of
the country including London St Pancras, York, Birmingham, Leicester and Nottingham.
The Derwent Valley Line runs between Derby-Belper-Cromford-Matlock Bath-Matlock
08457 484950 www.nationalrail.co.uk

By coach

National Express operate regular coach services to Derby from many parts of the country
0870 808080 www.nationalexpress.com

Derby Tourist Information Centre: 01332 255802.

Matlock Tourist Information Centre: 01629 583388.

Matlock Bath Tourist Information Centre: 01629 55082.

Where to Stay

Willersley Castle, nr. Cromford 01629 582270 www.christianguild.co.uk/willersley

Mount Tabor House B & B nr. Matlock 01773 857008 www.mountabor.co.uk

The Stuart Hotel, Derby 01332 340633 www.thestuart.com

Opposite: The Iron Bridge: the first bridge constructed from iron in the world.

Ironbridge Gorge

The Birthplace of the Industrial Revolution

Date of Inscription 1985

Why is this a World Heritage Site?

The Industrial Revolution precipitated a huge sea-change in the world economy and this valley was its crucible. The Iron Bridge itself is an iconic and enduring symbol of that revolution, the surrounding area having all the components to enable the region's development as an industrial centre. Here were the building bricks which fuelled the rapid growth of Britain's wealth, influence and empire in the 18th and 19th centuries. Many vital technological breakthroughs occurred here which were then disseminated throughout the globe. Since 1968 the Ironbridge Museum Trust has been a true pioneer in the field of industrial archaeology and heritage conservation.

Location

Ironbridge is in east Shropshire a few miles south of Telford and about 20 miles (30 kms) north west of Birmingham.

HISTORY

The gorge with its profuse supply of raw materials and good transport links down the River Severn to the Bristol Channel witnessed the production of iron since Henry VIII's time. Iron was crucial to the success of the Industrial Revolution – every new process needed iron, from the spinning mules for cotton mills, to boilers for steam engines. Later, the railway lines and ships that took Britain's manufactured goods to the world were all, of course, made of iron.

The importance of the contribution made by the Darby family in the 18th century (see box) cannot be overstated. At Ironbridge they transformed the science of iron manufacture.

Ironbridge Gorge boasts an incredible collection of factories, workshops, warehouses and canals together with ironmasters' and their workers' houses and public buildings – all crowned by the spectacle of the world's first iron bridge spanning the River Severn. Now that heavy industry has ceased, the natural beauty of the landscape has returned – the trees that were cut down to fuel furnaces have regenerated and the spoil tips from the mines have now been reclaimed by nature. The River Severn is clean and the smells and sounds of industry are no more.

WHAT TO SEE

The World Heritage Site is spread over 2 miles (3.6 km) in the narrow Severn valley downstream from its confluence with Caldebrook River in Coalbrookdale. There are currently 10 museums in an area of about 6 square miles; a car is needed to travel between them or you can use the Gorge Connect Shuttle Bus which is free to all Museum Passport holders. There are five main areas of interest from west to east:

THE DARBY FAMILY

Three generations of the Darby family – all called Abraham – were instrumental in creating a prototypical industrial centre at Ironbridge and Coalbrookdale.

Abraham Darby I (1678–1717) was born of Quaker parentage in Staffordshire and after an apprenticeship in Birmingham he moved to Bristol where, together with other Quakers, he set up a brass foundry at Baptist Mills just outside the city. Here the first steps were taken in new techniques using sand moulds for the casting of iron as well as brass goods. These techniques, developed with fellow Quaker John Thomas, facilitated new working methods enabling an early form of mass production which lowered the unit cost; before this each item had to be individually cast. In 1708 Darby patented these sand-casting techniques but it seems that his partners in Bristol were unwilling to continue to finance a venture they considered to be risky, so he decided to find premises at Coalbrookdale where he knew low-sulphur coal could be easily mined as it was near the surface. Darby then introduced another innovation, the use of coke, made from this low-sulphur coal to fire large furnaces (previously charcoal had been used). This enabled the manufacture of good quality castings of greater complexity, thinness and smoothness and led directly to the production of iron and brass steam engines.

His son, Abraham Darby II (1711–63), took his father's work a stage further by improving the coke-smelted pig iron so it could be used for intricate wrought-iron goods. Coalbrookdale began to gain a reputation as a place where the best iron goods could be made and by 1758 more than 100 Newcomen cylinders for steam engines had been cast there.

It was Abraham III (1750–91) who was to set the seal on his family's achievements by erecting the world's first cast-iron bridge in 1779, a 30 metres (100 ft) structure that still spans the River Severn.

Today the houses where the family lived (Rosehill House and Dale House) are open to view at Coalbrookdale and include the wood-panelled study in Dale House where Abraham Darby III worked on his plans for the bridge.

COALBROOKDALE

Abraham Darby developed his iron production techniques here in 1709 during Queen Anne's reign. The manufacture of iron was to become a driving force in the Industrial Revolution. By the 19th century the Coalbrookdale foundries had become very prosperous and their goods were exported as far away as New Zealand and Hawaii.

Today the Great Warehouse houses an Iron Museum that celebrates the history of early iron-making and clearly explains the processes with models and exhibits.

'Scene of superfluous grace, and wasted bloom, Oh violated Coalbrook!'
Anna Seward c. 1785

On the same site is the Long Warehouse with huge cast-iron columns which allowed railway carriages to be shunted underneath and loaded from above. The Old Furnace is preserved in a modern structure and is where in 1709 Abraham Darby first smelted iron using coke instead of charcoal. It is known as the Old Furnace because it was already over 50 years old when it was taken over by Darby. Behind the Old Furnace is the dam that holds back the Upper Furnace Pool from which water was harnessed to drive machinery.

On the hillside just above the railway viaduct are the elegant Ironmasters'

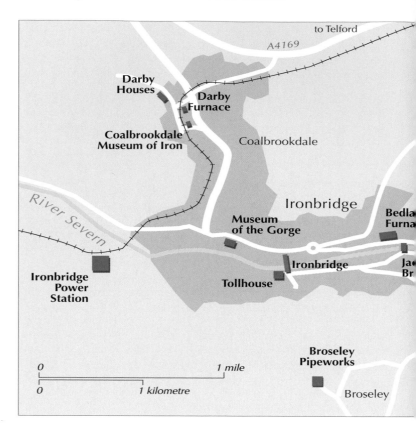

houses where the Darbys lived. They are open to the public and show Darby family pictures and objects, papers, and original furniture still in place.

On the other side of the valley are workers' terraces, known as Carpenters' Row with their original glazing and wooden shutters and a Wesleyan Methodist chapel.

IRONBRIDGE

It was here that mining for coal and minerals began in the 17th century when the

> '...the noises of the forges, mills, etc., with all their vast machinery, the flames bursting from the furnaces with the burning of the coal and the smoak of the lime kilns, are altogether sublime.'
> **Arthur Young c. 1775**

whole gorge was called Coalbrookdale. It was only later that the small town took its name from the bridge. The coal deposits in the region were near to the surface and in 1635 annual production from Broseley and Benthall was about 100,000 tons. Remains of two 18th-century blast furnaces, the Bedlam Furnaces, can be seen a short distance away from the modern town of Ironbridge.

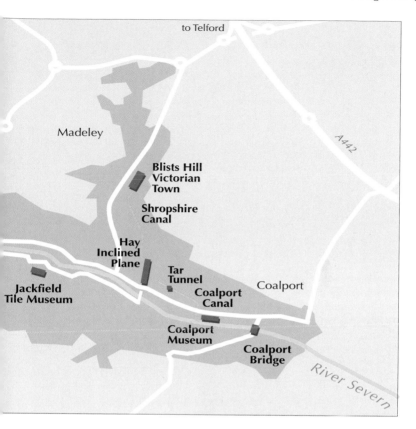

THE BUILDING OF THE IRON BRIDGE

In 1776 the nearest bridge over the River Severn was over 2 miles away at Buildwas. Although there were six ferry crossings in the gorge for people and goods it was an unpredictable, difficult and dangerous way of crossing the river, especially during the winter when it could become swollen, or during the summer months when it ran too shallow. In 1776 an Act of Parliament enabled the building of another bridge.

Thomas Farnolls Pritchard was the designer of its elegant lines; its arch spans 30.6 metres (100.5 ft) and it has five arch ribs which were each cast in two halves at the foundry. As such a construction had never been attempted before, they used the traditional woodworking dovetail method of the era to connect the cast-iron pieces. The dovetails, wedges and mortice-and-tenon joints used may account for the bridge's resistance to geological pressure due to the 'give' in them. The largest components were the half-ribs which each weigh about 5.25 tons. In all the bridge was made up of 800 castings of 12 basic types. It was a major feat to cast, move and raise these huge structures. The cost amounted to £6,000.

The world's first iron bridge was completed in 1779 but there was a long delay before it was open to traffic. When it was finally officially opened on New Year's Day 1781 it created a sensation and people flocked to see it – including many industrial spies.

The Iron Bridge showing the beautifully elegant design constructed using the same techniques as those in large-scale carpentry.

THE TOLL HOUSE AND THE MUSEUM OF THE GORGE

The exhibits explain the history and the significance of the building of the Iron Bridge. The museum has a giant scale model showing how the gorge appeared in 1796.

THE BROSELEY PIPEWORKS

Broseley had been well known for its clay pipes since the 17th century. This abandoned factory, a few miles south of Ironbridge, dates from the last half of the 19th century and was restored in 1993. It is now transformed into an evocative museum showing how clay pipes were made. The clay came from Devon and Cornwall and the finished pipes were then despatched throughout the country. However, the fashion for cigarettes meant that pipe sales dwindled after the First World War. The factory was closed in 1957 and left virtually untouched – a 'time capsule' until its restoration.

JACKFIELD

Jackfield is one of the oldest centres for ceramic production in the county and probably dates back to the 16th century. Coal mining and clay production (the local clay was perfect for tile making) were also important and it was the major port within the gorge. In 1756 there were 87 barges in active operation. For a while during the middle of the 19th century this small village was the world centre for the manufacture of tiles.

Tile Museum

This is located on the south side of the Ironbridge Gorge and celebrates the golden age of Victorian tiles with splendid displays in authentic settings. The tiles ended up in many exotic places, from Russian palaces to grand colonial buildings, as well as featuring on the walls of many Victorian public lavatories.

The decorative tiles industry greatly expanded in 1852 when the Maw family moved their works from Worcester as they found the Shrophire clays were more suitable for this type of tile.

The site was then taken over by a Yorkshire entrepreneur, Henry Powell Dunhill, and a new factory was erected in 1874. Dunhill was a Nonconformist dedicated to the welfare of his workers, establishing a reading room for them and instigating a profit-sharing scheme.

Blist's Hill

This large open-air museum near to the Shropshire Canal recreates a Victorian town and is staffed by people in period costume. Visitors can enter the houses and shops and see displays of tallow candle-making, watch a blacksmith or carpenter and even pop into the pub. There is a typical worker's cottage complete with vegetable garden, pigs and chickens while inside a fire blazes in the kitchen range.

Industrial remnants can be seen such as winding engines, shafts with their head frames and blast furnaces. The canal was linked to the River Severn by the Hay Inclined Plane (see below).

The candle maker at work at Blist's Hill.

Coalport

This town is also spanned by an iron bridge inspired by the original at Ironbridge but with a more streamlined design. It is still open to traffic.

The town's importance lies in the china and porcelain factory that was founded by John Rose at the end of the 18th century when the canal and Hay Inclined Plane made Coalport a transport hub. It was called 'Coalport' because this is where coal needed for the kilns was transferred from canal to river. There was also a local supply of fireclays used for the production of 'saggars' – the earthenware boxes inside which china is fired in the kilns.

John Rose owned one factory producing porcelain and his brother, Thomas, ran

The bottle kilns, workshops and warehouses at Coalport.

another on the other side of the canal. In 1814 the two companies were merged and the factory began to gain a high reputation for its artistry and quality.

In 1926 the factory at Coalport was closed after years of decline and Coalport China became part of the Wedgwood Group. However, the original buildings survived and in 1976 became a museum for the national collection of Coalport china, one of the 10 museums in the gorge. The light-filled low buildings of the factories and the bottle ovens which house the kilns still survive.

THE HAY INCLINED PLANE

This can be found about 180 metres (600 ft) upstream from the canal towpath at Coalport. In 1788 the owners of the Shropshire Canal held a competition for the 'best means of raising and lowering heavy weights from one navigation to another'.

The winners of the contest were Henry Williams and James Loudon and the incline was completed in 1793. The Inclined Plane (see left) is 305 metres (330 yds) long and has a vertical rise of over 61 metres (200 ft)

Blaenavon
Industrial Landscape

A Location forged from Iron, Coal and Steam

Date of Inscription 2000

Why is this a World Heritage Site?

The whole of Blaenavon and the surrounding areas are a perfect surviving example of the industrial heritage of South Wales which, in the 19th century, was the world's major centre for the production of iron and coal. The mines, the pit, the quarries, the primitive railway systems that criss-crossed the town, the furnaces, and also the miners' homes are all still to be seen in the 21st century. Its distinctive character was forged by the close relationship between the coal and iron industry and the workers who toiled in the pits and stoked the furnaces. Blaenavon was also at the forefront of new technology in iron and steel manufacture, the secrets of which emigrants from Wales passed all over the world.

Location

Blaenavon is approximately 25 miles (40 km) from the Welsh capital, Cardiff, in the north-eastern corner of the Welsh Valleys in Gwent.

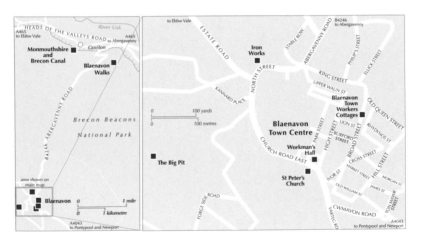

HISTORY

Iron ore was extracted from the mountains of Blaenavon as early as 1675 but few people lived there and the site was mainly used for grazing sheep. Everything changed when Lord Abergavenny, who owned the land, leased it to three entrepreneurs in 1788: Thomas Hill, Thomas Hopkins and Benjamin Pratt. They recognised the potential for a great ironworks. The site had all the mineral deposits necessary for the task (iron, coal, fireclay and limestone) in one place.

A year later three blast furnaces, using steam power, had transformed 'Lord Abergavenny's Hills'. It was the second largest ironworks in Wales and one of the largest in the world. The tiny original population was joined by an army of migrant workers from rural Wales, from the industrial Midlands and from Ireland and Scotland.

Whatever the Blaenavon Company needed to make iron was created in the valley which became a jungle of iron-ore workings, coal mines, iron forges, limestone quarries, railway tracks and housing for workers and their families.

In the 1860s the company built a new steelworks across the valley at Forgeside rendering the original works partially redundant (contributing to its value as a prime example of its original era). Blaenavon led the world again in the use of a modification of the Bessemer process crucial in the production of steel (see box below). Big Pit was sunk to serve the new works and growing prosperity came to the town enabling the erection of new public buildings such as the Workmen's Hall and Institute.

By 1891 the population in Blaenavon had grown to over 11,000 but the importance of steel was overtaken by coal. In Wales coal mining peaked in 1913 and roughly a quarter of Welshmen were employed in the industry. Big Pit was enlarged and when the British coal industry was nationalised in 1947 it was expanded further. However, steel production had ceased altogether by 1938 and Big Pit, the last large working colliery, closed in 1980. After a period of stagnation, new industries and the World Heritage Site citation have brought new life to Blaenavon and its people.

Sidney Gilchrist Thomas (1850-1885)

Thomas was born in London and worked there as a police court clerk but in his spare time studied chemistry. His aim was to solve the problem of eliminating phosphorus (a major impurity in some iron ores) from pig iron. Together with his cousin, Percy Gilchrist who worked at Blaenavon, he carried out a series of experiments to develop linings for Bessemer converters that could combine with phosphorus and thus eliminate it as slag. Edward Martin, the manager of the works, helped them and in 1878 the first public announcement of the discovery was made and a patent taken out. The process was soon in use throughout Britain and later in France, Belgium, Germany and Russia.

Andrew Carnegie paid $250,000 for the right to use the process in the US and said, 'These two young men, Thomas and Gilchrist of Blaenavon, did more for Britain's greatness than all the Kings and Queens put together. Moses struck the rock and brought forth water. They struck the useless phosphoric ore and transformed it into steel.'

Blaenavon Ironworks

Key Sites

This was once the most advanced ironworks in the world and today it is the best preserved 19th-century works in the world. The remains of six blast furnaces, operated by steam power, show 18th- and 19th-century ironmaking technology and its development better than any other area in Britain. Close by is a range of ruined kilns.

An impressive part of the site is the water balance tower (see photograph on page 136) which was erected in 1839. This technology used the power of water to counter-balance loads of pig iron raising them to a tram road and on to the forge at Garnddyrys on the other side of the mountain.

A view of the Ironworks, once the most advanced in the world.

A cast-iron frame bore a pulley wheel over which a chain linked a pair of lift cages each holding a cast-iron water tank. By piping water in or out of the tank, wagons could be lifted or lowered as needed. The ruined tower is a poignant symbol of Blaenavon's industrial heritage.

Stack Square and Engine Row

Close to the Ironworks these stone cottages were built in the late 18th century for the skilled workers who operated the furnaces. They form a square in the centre of which can be seen the base of the chimney stack for the 1860 engine house. The middle row of houses was first used as the company's office, shop and manager's house.

Pig Iron

The name is derived from the time when molten iron ran into moulds in sand beds fed from a common runner. The shape of the pinkish ingots branching off the oblong runner reminded the furnace men of a litter of piglets feeding from a sow. The individual ingots were referred to as pigs and the runner was called the sow - from this comes 'pig iron'.

Big Pit

This now houses the National Mining Museum of Wales and the buildings on the surface remain almost exactly as they were when mining ended in 1980.

Visitors can follow in the footsteps of the miners by taking an underground tour. They are lowered in a cage in the original 1860 mine shaft to see the early workings, some of which date from the 1830s. Above ground on the hillside are the miners' baths and canteen which was opened in 1939 in the international Modernist Style chosen by the Miners' Welfare Committee.

THE LANDSCAPE NORTH OF THE IRONWORKS

The bleak open hillsides are covered with important historical monuments which help show how the coal, iron ore, fireclay and limestone were gathered to enable the ironworks to function. The Tourist Information Centre has information on themed trails which explain the significance of the remains.

BRECKNOCK AND ABERGAVENNY CANAL (PART OF THE MONMOUTHSHIRE AND BRECON CANAL)

The canal was constructed between 1797 and 1812 and its outstanding feature is the basin at Lanfoist, the terminus of the primitive railway which brought the material from the ironworks to be loaded onto the canal boats. The railway trucks were usually pulled by horses. Over the canal is a bridge built of cast-iron plates carried on cast-iron T-shaped girders which is now used by canal boats. Walkers and cyclists can enjoy the peaceful towpaths.

BLAENAVON TOWN

Without a doubt Blaenavon is the best preserved iron town in Wales. Nineteenth-century terraces of iron and coal workers' cottages can be seen as well as many chapels such as Bethlehem, Horeb and Moriah. The Nonconformist chapels were a focus of education as well as religion and helped foster the identity of much of the Welsh-speaking workforce. They were also instrumental in fostering the great tradition of Welsh choirs. In the late 19th century the chapels' role was often taken over by working men's institutes.

ST PETER'S CHURCH

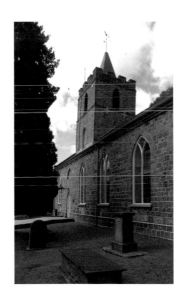

Built in 1804 in the Gothic revival style by the iron masters, Thomas Hill and Samuel Hopkins, as a gift to the town. Thomas Hill is buried in a vault by the church. Iron could be said to be the theme of the church – the font is made of cast-iron and the galleries are supported by cast-iron columns. In the quiet graveyard are five iron-topped chest tombs (see in the foreground of the photograph to the right). St Peter's school and the Ty Mawr mansion for the ironmaster are nearby.

WORKMEN'S HALL

The grandest building in the town is Blaenavon's Workmen's Hall and Institute which was opened in 1895. £10,000 was raised by a levy of a halfpenny a week deducted from the wages of the miners and ironworkers who also volunteered to help in its construction. It included a library, a reading room, and space for billiards, indoor games such as chess and draughts plus a stage for lectures and concerts – all for the working man.

Visitor Information

Tourist information centre 01495 792615 www.blaenavontic.com
www.world-heritage-blaenavon.org.uk

Opening times

Stack Square and Engine Row

Easter – October
Monday – Friday 9.30 am – 4.30 pm; Saturday 10 am – 5 pm; Sunday 10 am – 4.30 pm

01495 792615 www.blaenavontic.com

Big Pit

Mid-February – 30 November, Daily 9.30 am – 5 pm
Underground tours 10 am – 3.30 pm

01495 790311 www.nmgw.ac.uk

How to get there

By car:

From Birmingham and North – M5 South – leave at Junction 8 and continue on M50 to Ross on Wye. Take A40 to Abergavenny. At roundabout take second exit onto A465. Leave A465 at first exit and follow signs to Blaenavon and 'Big Pit'.

From London and South West – M4 West and leave at Junction 25A (Newport). Take A4042 as far as Pontypool. At roundabout (McDonalds Restaurant) take first exit and follow A4043 to Blaenavon.

By rail:

Links to Newport from London Paddington, Bristol and Cardiff and to Abergavenny from Birmingham New Street and Manchester Piccadilly.

By bus:

Route No X24, 23, 30 Newport – Blaenavon, Route X4 Abergavenny – Brynmawr, then Route 30 Brynmwr – Blaenavon or X3 Abergavenny – Pontypool, then X24 Pontypool – Blaenavon.

Where to stay

Parkway Hotel, Cwmbran 01633 871199 www.bw-parkwayhotel.co.uk

Rutland Cottage B & B, Pontypool 01495 772222 www.rutlandcottagebandb.co.uk

Llansantffraed Court Hotel nr. Abergavenny 01873 840678 www.llch.co.uk

Opposite: Beaumaris Castle, overlooking the Menai Straits
with the mountains of Snowdonia in the background.

Castles and Town Walls of Edward I in Gwynedd

The Ring of English Fortresses surrounding the Heart of Wales

Date of Inscription 1986

Why are they a World Heritage Site?

The castles and fortified towns of Gwynedd are the finest examples of late 13th-century and early 14th-century military architecture in Europe. They have undergone only minimal restoration and provide a superb repository of medieval architectural forms in a stunning landscape.

Location

The castles, towns and walls of Caernarfon, Conwy, Beaumaris and Harlech are located in the former principality of Gwynedd in north Wales.

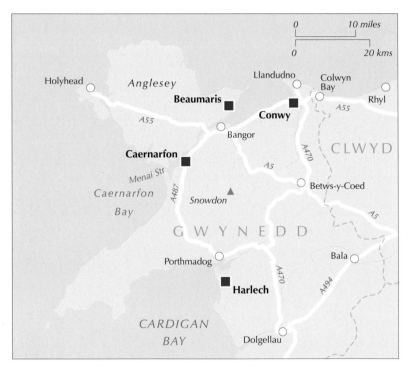

History

Edward I (1272–1307) strove throughout his reign to expand and defend his territory. He would not countenance Welsh independence and waged war against them in several campaigns from 1276. To aid his subjugation of Wales he built more than ten castles, including the four cited in the World Heritage inscription. Even now, the iron ring of immense fortresses surrounding the coastal fringes of Snowdonia that stretch from Flint to Aberystwyth remind everyone of the oppression of the Welsh by the English. The expense of building them was huge – it is estimated, from the records that still remain, that the king must have spent more than ten times his annual income on the work.

All four of the cited castles were built by James of St George, the master military architect of his age, which explains the coherence of their design. Masons, carpenters, labourers and woodcutters were impressed from all over the kingdom to work on these great fortifications, including 40 diggers and 10 carpenters from as far afield as Northumberland and 15 masons and 25 carpenters from Gloucestershire. They gathered in Chester and were then dispersed to different sites.

Conwy Castle and Walls

Overlooking the Conwy estuary, the castle with its eight towers is one of the most impressive fortresses in Wales. It was built between 1283–87, its layout dictated by the shape of the rock on which it is situated. It is an elongated structure with two barbicans and a great bow-shaped hall in the outer ward with the inner ward housing the royal apartments. Building work began early in June 1283 and between then and 1284 sums amounting to over £5,800 were paid by the keeper of the Wardrobe to the clerk of works and the master, James of St George.

The town walls are three-quarters of a mile in length and are one of the most complete examples of their type in Europe. They are remarkable for their state of preservation, forming a near complete circuit around the town. Only a small section near the quay is inaccessible, and even here, the ruins of the wall have been incorporated into existing buildings. The walls are flanked by 21 towers and three double tower gateways north and west of the castle.

The building of town walls was pivotal to Edward's policy of subjugating the local population. The castle towns were inhabited by English settlers who could form a militia if the need arose. The Welsh population were kept separate and could only enter the towns during the day. A market within the walls was granted by royal charter in 1284 which ensured that the town's economy was under the dominion of the English.

A view of Conwy Castle, showing the encompassing town walls.

THE WAR AGAINST THE WELSH

- **1267** Llwywelyn ap Gruffydd recognised by Henry III as Prince of Wales but on the accession of Edward I Llwywelyn refuses to acknowledge his obligations as vassal to the new king

- **1276–77** Edward marches on Wales with a force of 15,000

- **1277** After his capture in Snowdonia Llwywelyn is forced to accept the Peace of Aberconway

- **1279** Llwywelyn marries Eleanor, daughter of Simon de Monfort, with Edward's blessing at Worcester Cathedral. Edward pays for the ceremony

- **1282** The Welsh rise in revolt again, led by Llwywelyn's brother David. Llwywelyn joins his brother and leads the Welsh resistance against Edward's invasion

- **11 December 1282** Llwywelyn is killed by the English in a skirmish at Irfon Bridge near Builth Wells. Llwywelyn's lands are seized by Edward and he gives his own son, the future Edward II, the title of Prince of Wales

- **1283** Edward begins his castle-building programme

Caernarfon Castle

Caernarfon was the ancient centre of Gwynedd, and its occupation by Edward's forces in 1283 following the death of Llwywelyn in battle was the culmination of the war. The castles of Llwywelyn's brother David were besieged and David was captured and executed, leaving Edward to savour his total victory over the last Welsh prince of Wales.

The castle at Caernarfon was probably commissioned during these tumultuous events as the centre of a new order. The king intended the castle to be a royal residence and seat of government for north Wales. Its symbolic status was ensured

A view of the lower and upper wards of Caernarfon Castle.

when Edward's son was born there and became the first English Prince of Wales in 1284. In 1969 the castle was the setting for the investiture of HRH Prince Charles as Prince of Wales.

In 1294 the Welsh rose in revolt again, captured the castle and sacked it. In the six months Caernarfon remained in the rebels' hands grave damage was done to its fabric and the surrounding walls. Edward's response was to commission the building of Beaumaris in Anglesey, and in 1295, after the English regained control of Caernarfon, to resume building operations and repairs to the castle. Experienced masons were sought and orders were sent to the justiciars of Chester 'to cause 100 suitable masons experienced in such work as the king is engaged upon at Kaernaruan to be chosen in the town of Chester… and to cause them to come with their tools to Kaernaruan without delay.'

Although there are many similarities with the plan of Conwy Castle, Caernarfon was built to look different from the other castles and has polygonal, rather than round, towers; the walls are patterned with bands of differently coloured stone.

Harlech Castle

The Welsh stronghold of Castell y Bere fell in April 1283 and a force of 560 infantry led by Sir Otto de Grandson marched from there to Harlech to begin preparations for the building of the castle. Once again an army of labourers, craftsmen and masons worked over the next seven years under the direction of James of St George. The final result was a compact and perfectly concentric castle with one line of defences enclosed by another. Today the outer wall is in ruins and the full strength of the original fortress is difficult to envisage.

A remarkable feature of the castle is the gated and fortified stairway plunging almost 61 metres (200 ft) to the foot of the castle rock. The high tide level of

Harlech Castle from the south west with the distant mountains of Snowdonia as its backdrop.

Tremadog Bay has now receded but this once gave the castle's inhabitants access to supplies from the sea and during the Welsh rising of 1294 this proved to be a lifeline for the garrison as ships from Ireland were able to furnish them with provisions.

With its four round corner towers and twin-tower gatehouse Harlech Castle rises proudly from the rocks on which it is sited, an impregnable fortress overlooking the sea and all of the land between it and the distant mountains of Snowdonia. Even if attackers reached the gatehouse they were presented with a formidable challenge by the castle's intricate web of gates, portcullis and arrow slits.

In 1404 Harlech Castle, built by an English king to conquer the Welsh, was captured by Owen Glendower and became the focus of his rebellion against Henry IV. During the English Civil War it was also the last Royalist stronghold to fall to the Parliamentarians.

Beaumaris Castle

An unfinished masterpiece, this would have been the largest of Edward's castles and was once again designed by his master mason James of St George. It is a perfect example of a concentrically planned castle – walls within walls, all surrounded by a moat which is regularly filled by tidal water. The gate next-the-sea entrance protected the tidal dock which allowed supply ships to sail right up to the castle.

The Welsh revolt of September 1294 which had resulted in the occupation of Caernarfon Castle, also had repercussions on Anglesey. The island's sheriff, Sir Roger Pilsdon, was a prominent victim and so the reoccupation of the island was vital to Edward's plans. The necessary decisions were made at a council in Worcester and shortly afterwards Sir Henry Latham of Lancashire was ordered to sail in his galley for the island in command of a force of 500 men carried in 12 ships. Among

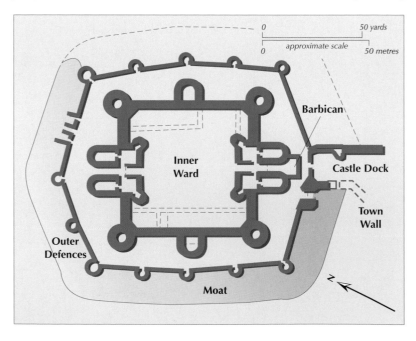

Materials used in 1295 to build Beaumaris Castle

2428 tons of sea-coal for burning lime

640 quarters of charcoal

42 masons' axes

3277 boards

8 loads of lead

160 pounds of tin

314 'bends' of iron

105,000 assorted nails

the men sailing were 50 diggers and 21 carpenters to start work on the castle.

Work proceeded swiftly into 1295 using vast quantities of stone and wood as well as other materials (see box). In July Edward came to inspect the work and was able to stay on site in a temporary thatched-roofed building. However, over the next few years, Edward turned his attention to his northern neighbour and money and resources began to be diverted from Wales to Scotland.

The defences include numerous ingeniously sited arrow slits, and the entrances are protected by murder holes from which substances such as hot oil could be poured over enemy forces. Any attackers would have met 14 separate obstacles and four lines of fortification resulting from the 'walls within walls' design.

The moat and outer defences at Beaumaris on the island of Anglesey.

The squatness of the castle's outline is the result of its unfinished state. The conquest of Wales was nearly over and the sense of urgency had gone. The great towers of the inner ward are still without their top storeys, while the turrets were never so much as begun.

However, the castle is still a formidable sight lying on the 'beau marais' 'beautiful marsh' in a scenic setting on the island of Anglesey.

VISITOR INFORMATION

It is possible to buy a World Heritage Explorer Pass for admission to all four castles. They are available at any of the castle's entrances. The pass also includes admission to the World Heritage Site at Blaenavon Ironworks (see page 137).

CONWY CASTLE AND WALLS

OPENING TIMES
Open daily from 9.30 am – 5 pm; June–September until 6 pm
Winter openings daily 9.30 – 4 pm; Sundays 11 am – 4 pm
Closed 24 – 26 December and 1 January
01443 336000 www.cadw.wales.gov.uk

HOW TO GET THERE
Conwy is on the A55 or B5106.
Train: It is about a mile and half from Llandudno Junction on the Crewe–Llandudno Junction/Holyhead line.
National Rail Enquiries: 08457 484950 From abroad: 44 (0) 20 7278 5240
www.nationalrail.co.uk

CAERNARFON CASTLE

OPENING TIMES AND CONTACT INFORMATION
See above.

HOW TO GET THERE
Caernarfon is on the A405, A487 and B4366.
The nearest railway station is at Bangor about 10 miles away.
National Rail Enquiries: see above.

HARLECH CASTLE
OPENING TIMES AND CONTACT INFORMATION
See above.

HOW TO GET THERE
Harlech is on the A496.
Train: Harlech is on the Shrewsbury – Machynlleth/Pwllheli line.
National Rail Enquiries: see above.

BEAUMARIS CASTLE

OPENING TIMES AND CONTACT INFORMATION
See above.

HOW TO GET THERE
A545 (Menai Bridge).
There are limited local rail services on the island – trains run through the southern part of the islands from Llanfairpwll to Holyhead. Bangor Station is about nine miles away.

WHERE TO STAY

CONWY

Castle Bank Hotel 01492 593888 www.castle-bank.co.uk
Quay Hotel 01492 564100 www.quayhotel.com
Gwynedd Guest House 01492 596537

CAERNARFON

Celtic Royal Hotel 01286 674477 www.celtic-royal.co.uk
Ty'n Rhos Country House 01248 670489 www.tynrhos.co.uk
Isfryn Guesthouse 01286 675628

HARLECH

Castle Cottage Hotel 01766 780479 www.castlecottageharlech.co.uk
Morlyn Guest House 01341 241298
Hotel Maes-y-Neuadd 01766 780200 www.neuadd.com

BEAUMARIS

Ye Olde Bulls Head Inn 01248 810329 www.bullsheadinn.co.uk
The Bishopsgate House Hotel 01248 810302 www.bishopsgatehousehotel.co.uk
Plas Cichle 01248 810488

North of England

Durham Castle and Cathedral

Frontiers of the Roman Empire:
Hadrian's Wall

Liverpool – Maritime Mercantile City

Saltaire

Studley Royal Park
including the ruins of Fountains Abbey

Opposite: The great towers of Durham Cathedral rise above the River Wear.

Durham Castle and Cathedral

A Sublime Example of Medieval Architecture

Date of Inscription 1986

Durham Cathedral was built to house the relics of St Cuthbert, the saint who brought Christianity to Northumbria, and those of the great chronicler and monk, the Venerable Bede. The present building was erected in the late 11th and early 12th centuries and is the largest and finest example of Norman church architecture in England, illustrating the importance of the Benedictine monastic community at that time. The castle, built at the behest of William the Conqueror in 1072, stands behind the cathedral, a defensive citadel against the incursions of the Scots.

The awesome sight of the cathedral and castle perched high above the River Wear on a precipitous rock face is one of the wonders of medieval Europe. Its early name was Dun Holm from the Anglo-Saxon, which meant the island on the hill.

Location

Durham is in the north east of England, about 15 miles south west of Sunderland. County Durham was for centuries a semi-autonomous palatinate, outside the English political and legal system.

BACKGROUND HISTORY

The city's history goes back many thousands of years but its defining moment came when the body of St Cuthbert of Lindisfarne came to Durham in 995. In order to keep his precious remains safe from Viking raids they were moved from Holy Island, first to Chester-le-Street, then Ripon and finally to Durham. A shrine was built in a wooden church on top of the rocky hill protected on three sides by the River Wear and easily defensible on the fourth side. It is thought that this church occupied the site of the present church of St Mary le Bow. The wooden structure was soon replaced with a minster built of stone and in 1022 Cuthbert's remains were joined by the relics of the Venerable Bede from Jarrow.

After the Norman conquest of 1066 the site of Durham was chosen for the building of a castle and cathedral. The one remaining adversary that the Normans faced in Britain was the Scots and this fortress was ideal for defensive purposes. William the Conqueror ordered the castle to be built on his way back from a foray against Malcolm III of Scotland and saw the area as a vital buffer against the Scots. In these circumstances the bishops of Durham were given the power by the king to govern the north of England on his behalf and assume the title of 'Prince Bishop'. They could raises taxes, mint coins and had supreme jurisdiction over both civil and military affairs.

The construction of the Norman cathedral in the Romanesque style began in 1093 and was completed only 40 years later. The pace at which it was built gave the

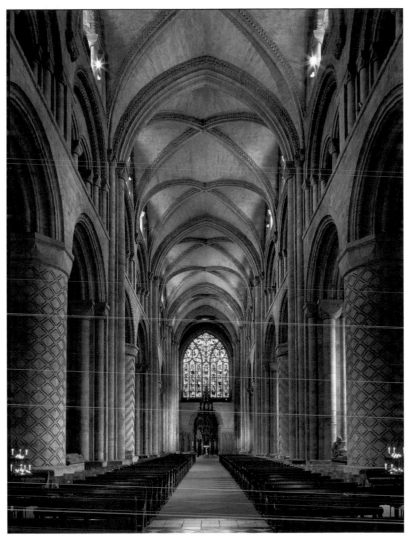

The Cathedral nave looking west.

cathedral its unity of style. The shrine of St Cuthbert made it a focus for pilgrims and the city became one of the richest in the kingdom. The imposing structures of cathedral and castle reinforced the twin powers of church and state.

THE CATHEDRAL

Durham Cathedral, unlike any other English cathedral of the time, was vaulted in stone from the outset. The massive bundle piers and huge cylindrical columns along the nave support the vaulted roof (which is strengthened using ribs which form shallow pointed arches) and all the arches of the arcades are marked by alternating diamond shapes and chevrons to give a strong sense of rhythm and harmony to

St Cuthbert (c.635–687)

The fragmentary information we have of Cuthbert's life comes from two contemporary biographies – one by Bede. Opinions differ as to where he was born, with Melrose and Dunbar cited as possible birthplaces, but it is more probable that he was born in Northumbria possibly of aristocratic parentage. As a young man he had a vision of the soul of St Aidan being carried to heaven by angels which prompted him to enter the monastery at Melrose where (after an interlude at the new monastery at Ripon) he became prior in 664. This coincided with the Synod of Whitby which settled the dispute between the Roman and Celtic forms of Christianity in England in favour of the former. Cuthbert then became prior of the religious community at Lindisfarne as it made the transition to Roman practices. He was noted not only for his piety, but for his gentleness and patience. In 676 he was given leave by the abbot to retreat to Farne Island but after a few years was called on to leave his life of contemplation and was ordained bishop of Lindisfarne at Easter 685. He retired again to Farne Island after a year and died there in 687. His remains were entombed on Lindisfarne and became a centre of pilgrimage and a place of miracles. When the remains were exhumed for translation to a shrine, legend has it that his body was perfectly preserved.

Cuthbert is associated with the illuminated Lindisfarne Gospels finished in the early eighth century and which may have been produced to further his cult. The Gospels can be seen at the British Museum but a modern facsimile is in the Treasury at Durham Cathedral.

the whole. It is believed that the builders may have been influenced by architecture seen in the eastern Mediterranean, and Norman-controlled Sicily, by returning crusaders. But the use of slightly pointed arches in the rib vaults may in turn have influenced masons in northern France where early forms of what is now known

as Gothic architecture appeared two decades later.

In 1170 a new Lady Chapel enclosed the Norman west door. This structure, known as the Galilee Chapel (see left), is unique to Durham (being at the west end of the cathedral) and has quite a different mood from the nave; heaviness gives way to airy elegance. The interior of the single-storey hall is divided into five aisles with wide arches ornamented with deep chevrons; oblique views are rewarded with a multitude of cross vistas. The remains of the Venerable Bede are buried here in a simple tomb.

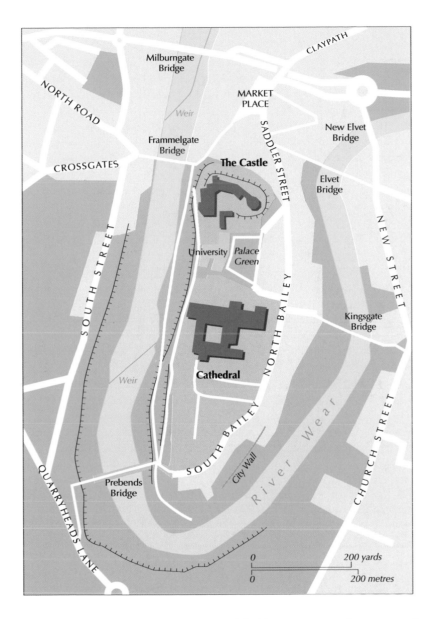

The 13th century saw the replacement of the Norman apse at the eastern end of the cathedral by the Chapel of the Nine Altars. This lofty chapel built in the Early English and Decorated styles rising to the same height as the main cathedral features fine craftsmanship especially in the vault patterns. St Cuthbert's shrine is situated here behind the High Altar. The Neville screen, separating St Cuthbert's shrine from the high altar, is carved from Caen Stone from Normandy. It was installed in 1380 and once housed 107 alabaster figures, the removal of which has perhaps allowed the delicate beauty of the screen to be better appreciated.

159

The towers of the cathedral are all massive. The western pair which were probably completed in about 1220 make a huge impact. From the 14th to the 17th centuries they had lead-covered spires but their present crowns date from 1801. The central tower is a 15th-century replacement for its Norman predecessor which was destroyed in a storm in 1429. It stands 67 metres (218 ft) high, a sentinel over the whole building.

To the south of the cathedral are the monastic buildings, the cloister and chapter house, unfortunately heavily restored in the 19th century. The Benedictine monastery suffered closure in 1539 under Henry VIII's dissolution programme, ending hundreds of years of monastic life at the cathedral. In 1540 the cathedral was refounded, the last prior becoming dean, and 12 former monks the first canons.

THE CASTLE

The castle was the palace of the Prince Bishops from the late 11th century up to the 1830s. Following the creation of Durham University in 1832 the castle became one of its first residential colleges, a use that remains to the present day.

The castle retains its original 11th-century plan of a motte or mound on which is a central keep with a large bailey to the east, within which were ranges of private and administrative buildings including the surviving Great Hall and kitchens. The long history of the Prince Bishops is reflected in the many changes to the castle itself and has resulted in a complex range of buildings rich in architectural history and interest. Of particular note is the remarkable survival of the Norman Chapel. It is a tiny room with three groined vaults. The decoration of its six capitals is seen as 'an essential reference in the study of sculpture after 1066 in England'. Also to be seen is the delicately carved stonework to Bishop Le Puiset's gallery and doorway, and Bishop Cosin's 'Black Staircase', which is one of the finest remaining late 17th-century staircases in the country. From the 18th century to the early 19th century the castle's exterior was extensively remodelled in an early form of the Gothic Revival style.

THE PRINCE BISHOPS

The massive castle and cathedral symbolised the extraordinary powers of Durham's Prince Bishops in the land between the Rivers Tyne and Tees which were the last vestiges of those once held by the kings and earls of the ancient kingdom of Northumbria.

Durham was a palatinate under the jurisdiction of the Prince Bishops and was not represented at Westminster until after the Civil War in the 17th century. English Palatinates were border regions (other areas with palatine powers include the earldom of Chester) where the need for security led to local rulers being given special powers including the right to levy taxes, raise troops and administer justice. Durham was never included in the Domesday survey and had fiercely resisted the Norman conquest of 1066 so when it was finally subdued its rulers were given palatine powers in order to control the local population as well as to protect the region against Scottish incursions.

In 1536 Henry VIII removed some of the bishops' legal powers but it was not until the Established Church Act of 1836 that the last palatine privileges were dissolved. However, even today the bishops of Durham, together with those of London and Winchester, still hold seniority over other bishops in the Church of England.

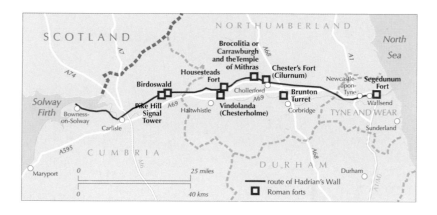

at Mons Graupius in Aberdeenshire in AD 83. But the Romans could not sustain this advance and the army withdrew to the Tyne–Solway isthmus around AD 100. A chain of forts connected by a road, the Stanegate, was built which marked the limit of occupation for about 20 years.

HADRIAN'S WALL

'The Britons could not be kept under control' according to a biographer of the Emperor Hadrian (117–138) and Hadrian therefore ordered the existing structures to be strengthened in 122 'to separate the Romans from the barbarians' by building a wall in stone in the eastern half of the isthmus. It was Aulus Platorius Nepos, the governor of Britain, who had the responsibility of carrying out the emperor's instructions. The finished Wall was a huge achievement – it took over 10 years to build with troops from every legion in Britain together with other other auxilliary personnel being used in the construction.

A V-shaped ditch was dug to the north of the Wall, up to 6 metres (19 ft) wide and 2 metres (6 ft) deep. A fortlet was built every Roman mile attached to the rear (south side) of the wall with gateways through from the north and south. These

RECENT FINDS

Impressive 1,800-year-old Roman remains relating to Hadrian's Wall are still being uncovered. In August 2008 two stone sarcophagi lying side by side were unearthed at a dig in Newcastle city centre. They are believed to have been used for the burial of members of a powerful family, perhaps a fort commander or other senior military man, from the adjacent walled fort of Pons Aelius close to where the city's railway station now stands. The Wall itself would have run to the north of this. Inside one of the sandstone sarcophagi the headless body of a young child was found; the other contained female remains. Futher discoveries on Forth Street include cremation urns, a cobbled Roman road, a Roman well and the foundations of Roman shops and homes.

David Heslop, Tyne and Wear County Archaeologist, noted: 'For the first time, we are starting to understand the layout of the civilian settlement that provided services to the garrison of the fort, and we can catch a glimpse of the Roman way of life, and death, on the northern frontier of the Empire.' All remains will become part of the Great North Museum collection.

The outline remains of Milecastle 42 on a lonely stretch of Hadrian's Wall, seen from Cawfield's Crag.

could house approximately eight soldiers, though some were larger. There were also turrets between each milecastle for observation and signalling purposes. Later, 16 forts were added which could each accommodate between 500 and 1000 soldiers – both cavalry and infantry. Enclosing these features to the south was a ditch known as the Vallum with a flat base and virtually sheer sides flanked by turf mounds which created a defensible zone behind the Wall.

Adjacent civilian settlements mushroomed near the forts to serve the needs of this concentration of men such as shops, taverns, bath houses, temples and workshops. Some of these grew into small towns beyond which cemeteries have been found.

Apart from damage following the Jacobite Uprising of 1745/6 when the government ordered the construction of a road, some of which lay on top of the Wall and entailed its destruction, much of the structure survives today. It offers 'an incomparable ensemble of defensive constructions and settlements in an archaeological zone that is no doubt the largest in the United Kingdom'. (Icomos)

WHAT TO SEE TODAY
SOUTH SHIELDS ARBEIA FORT
Situated four miles east of the end of the Wall, this fort once guarded the entrance to the River Tyne. It played an essential role as the military supply base for all the forts along the Wall. Today there is a museum displaying finds from the site. There are many excavated remains and excellent replicas of the original buildings.

SEGEDUNUM WALLSEND FORT
This is the most easterly outpost of the Wall standing on the River Tyne at the appropriately named Wallsend. Segedunum means 'strong fort'. The buildings include the commanding officer's house and headquarters, a hospital and soldiers' barracks.

There is a large interactive museum plus a tall viewing tower which gives an excellent perspective on the site, a reconstructed bath house and a length of Wall.

CORBRIDGE ROMAN TOWN

These remains of a series of Roman forts are about half a mile north west of the modern village of Corbridge. The first forts were established in AD 79-85 and Roman occupation continued into the 160s. Their importance hinged on their pivotal position at the junction of Stanegate Road which went to Carlisle and Dere Street which led south to London and north towards Scotland.

The extensive remains include a fountain house with an aqueduct, granaries and walled military compounds that surrounded houses, temples and a headquarters with an underground strongroom. The nearby museum offers displays of a rich variety of Roman artefacts and armour.

BRUNTON TURRET

An 8 ft high tower about 3 miles north of Corbridge may have been built by the men of the 20th Legion. At Chollerford there are extensive remains of Roman bridges over the Tyne.

CHESTER'S FORT ' CILURNUM'

This was built a quarter mile west of Chollerford in AD 123 and is the best-preserved Roman cavalry fort in Britain. It was constructed to protect the Roman bridge that carried the Wall, as well as the military road, over the River Tyne. The entire

Chester's Fort in the snow: the best-preserved Roman cavalry fort in Britain, built in AD 123.

foundations of the military buildings survive including the luxurious house of the commandant. By the river there are well-preserved steam rooms and bathing areas used by the garrison. Inscriptions which have been found on the site show that the army came from all over the empire including Dalmatia and Upper Rhineland. A museum displays a collection of Roman finds from statues and shoes to board games.

Brocolitia or Carrawburgh and the Temple of Mithras

This is the northernmost point of the Wall and lies in open moorland just over 1 mile west of Milecastle 30. The site was first excavated in the late 19th century when a military bath house was uncovered outside the west gate of the fort. It is thought that the Roman name for the Carrawburgh fort was Brocolitia – itself probably borrowed from the original Celtic meaning of Badger Holes.

A number of Roman and Celtic shrines have been found at this site. One unearthed in 1876 was to Coventina, a Celtic water goddess; once there was a sacred spring and pool here. Thousands of coins, pieces of jewellery, and pottery were found thrown by supplicants at the goddess's shrine. Some of these can be seen today at Chester's Fort Museum. A decade later came the discovery of another shrine dedicated to the local water nymphs.

In 1949 a temple to the god Mithras built about AD 200 was excavated. The original altars have been replaced by replicas – the originals can be found in the new Great North Museum in Newcastle upon Tyne. This temple appears to have been partly destroyed in the fourth century, perhaps by Christians who hated Mithraism as so many of its rituals were similar to their own (see box). The Temple of Mithras is one of three found along Hadrian's Wall. Excavated material from all three is exhibited at the Great North Museum.

At Carrawburgh worshippers entered the Mithraeum through a door leading to an antechamber that at one time housed an 'ordeal pit', used by followers to undergo the ordeals of heat, cold and fasting. A statuette of a mother goddess with a small pot for offerings was found in this area. A screen divided the

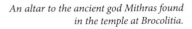

An altar to the ancient god Mithras found in the temple at Brocolitia.

THE CULT OF MITHRAS

The cult originated in India but the Roman army encountered it in Persia during the reign of the Emperor Nero (AD 54–68). Mithraism later became conflated with the cult of the invincible sun god Sol Invictus worshipped by soldiers. The story of the god's birth is often depicted showing him springing from a rock or from a tree but at Housesteads on the Wall he arrives bursting from a Cosmic Egg holding the sword of truth and torch of light in his upraised arms. Around him in an egg-shaped frame is the cosmos with the 12 signs of the zodiac – a unique representation of him in Britain.

Mithras captures a bull and kills it to release its lifeforce for mankind. This bull-slaying scene (tauroctony) is found in either a wall relief or painting in all Mithraic temples. Followers were divided into seven grades and each wore a costume and headmask to symbolise their status. They had to be initiated into each grade through severe tests in secret rituals. The religion was only open to men.

Mithraism has many similarities to Christianity. Mithras was born on 25 December, remained celibate, his worship involved baptism, the partaking of bread marked with a cross and wine as sacrificial blood, and his followers held Sundays sacred. Mithraists called themselves 'brother' and were led by a priest called 'father' (Pater).

antechamber from the nave of the temple where worshippers on benches would have taken part in the ritual meals which marked the initiation ceremonies. Three large altars were found in this sanctuary as well as smashed remains of a tauroctony (see box above). A ritual deposit of two pots containing the skull of a cockerel and two lumps of charcoal made from pinecones was found under the altars.

On one of the altars Mithras is depicted wearing a cloak and a radiating crown with its rays cut through to a hollow niche from which an oil lamp would have been placed so that light showed through the holes. The altars all carry dedications from Roman soldiers.

At Carrawburgh the Wall is seen at its scenic best, snaking over an undulating ridge above cliffs and lakes.

HOUSESTEADS FORT

Housesteads' was known as Vervovicium meaning 'the place of the fighters' and could accommodate between 800–1,000 men. It is the most complete Roman fort in Britain and spreads over a 2 hectare area (5 acres) with wonderful views of the surrounding

Part of the ruins of Housesteads Fort which was able to house up to a thousand soldiers.

moorland. It was first built between AD 120–125, then substantially rebuilt and enlarged under the rule of Emperor Septimus Severus *c.* 200. It boasts the ruins of a headquarters building, a commanding officer's house, granaries, barracks, a hospital and a multi-seated latrine, and it was here that the extraordinary sculpture of Mithras was found. Some houses of an accompanying civil settlement are visible outside the walls. There is also a museum which recreates the fort.

VINDOLANDA (CHESTERHOLME) AND ROMAN ARMY MUSEUM

One mile south of the Wall lies the remains of the garrison fort of Vindolanda. The name means white lawns or white fields. It is known that the Romans referred to it by this name because of an altar set up by the civilians at Vindolanda to the god Vulcan which was found during drainage work in 1914. The altar is on display in the museum.

Vindolanda was first garrisoned in the earliest phase of the establishment of Roman Britain's northern frontier, in the decades immediately preceding the building of Hadrian's Wall. In the first 40 years of its existence the fort seems to have undergone five stages of building and rebuilding in timber, before the establishment of the first stone-built fort by the mid-second century. Only a small area has been excavated, and the excavations still continue. One of the most exciting finds has been some 300 charred writing tablets discovered in the remains of the commander's house.

Apart from the commander's house there is a large bathhouse and the remains of civilian buildings. To help visitors visualise the fort there are lifesized mock-ups in wood and stone of the towers and wall.

A birthday invitation dated 11 September to Sulpicia Lepidina, the commandant's wife in c. AD 100 asking her to celebrate the birthday of Claudia Severa – this is one of the earliest known examples of a woman's handwriting in Latin.

BIRDOSWALD

High above the meandering River Irthing this fort, three turrets and two milecastles can all be seen on this stretch of the Wall. It was a base for 1,000 soldiers and was built on an earlier construction of turf. Three of the four main gateways, two granary buildings, worshops and a unique drill hall have all been excavated.

THE VINDOLANDA TABLETS

Unknown before this excavation at Vindolanda these tablets were locally produced from birch and alder wood. They are about the size of a modern postcard and about 1 mm thick; writing in ink covers one surface with the address on the opposite side. It is possible they were being burnt before the garrison left to fight in the Dacian wars.

The tablets give a unique insight into the thoughts and concerns of the inhabitants. The find is mainly made up of the correspondence of the commanding officer, Flavius Cerialis. Informal letters of greeting and friendship are found on the tablets; for instance, the prefect of the fort was in correspondence with the governor of the province, who was an occasional dinner guest at Vindolanda. The garrison was by no means utterly isolated – it was part of an army of about 50,000 in northern Britain and the Roman roads ensured rapid communication. London could be reached within a week.

Beyond the high-ranking officers and military clerks, ordinary soldiers were also using letters to exchange news, request presents and send thanks. There is a cook's diary detailing who had been to dinner and what dishes he had served, a birthday party invitation from one commandant's wife to another and many other intimate details of life at the fort.

PIKE HILL SIGNAL TOWER

The remains of one of a network of signal towers predating Hadrian's Wall, Pike Hill was later joined to the Wall at an angle of 45 degrees. Beside it is a later turret.

MARYPORT

Twenty miles past the end of the Wall at Bowness-on-Solway are the well-defined earthworks of Maryport Fort. It was initially founded in the first century and then rebuilt during Hadrian's reign. Next to it is an informative museum with the largest group of Roman military altar stones and inscriptions in Britain. The collection was begun in the 16th century by the Senhouse family and is of international importance.

RAVENGLASS BATH HOUSE

In the second century Ravenglass was a substantial Roman naval base known as Glannaventa. Little remains of the fort apart from the large and impressive bath house located outside the fort. Its walls still stand almost 4 metres (13ft) high. It is situated about a quarter of a mile east of Ravenglass.

THE TULLIE HOUSE MUSEUM, CARLISLE

The collections include a considerable amount of material from the western end of Hadrian's Wall and other Roman sites in North Cumbria, some relating to excavations carried out by English Heritage.

Visitor Information

The A69 runs a few miles to the south of the wall and connects the major north-south routes between England and Scotland: the A1M and A1 to the east and the M6 / A74M to the west. The B6318 follows the line of the Wall fairly closely for much of its length.

Birdoswald

On the B6318, a few miles north east of Brampton.
The Roman Army Museum is nearby at Greenhead.
Open daily 10.00 am – 5.30 pm, April – 30 September; closing at 4.00 pm in October.
It is possible to stay at a residential centre on the site. 01697 747602
www.english-heritage.org.uk

Brocolitia

Near the small village of Simonburn, north west of Hexham.

Chester's Fort 'Cilurnum'

Open daily 9.30 am – 6.00 pm, April to September; 10.00 am – 4.00 pm October – March.
Closed 24 – 26 December and 1 January.   www.english-heritage. org.uk

Corbridge Roman Town

Open daily 10.00 am – 5.30 pm, 21 March – 30 September; 10.00 am – 4.00 pm, 1 – 31 October. 1 November – 31 March open Saturdays and Sundays 10.00 am – 4.00 pm
Closed 24 – 26 December and 1 January.   www.english-heritage.org.uk

Great North Museum, Newcastle upon Tyne

Includes a Hadrian's Wall Gallery. Open daily 10.00 am – 5.00 pm Mondays – Saturdays; 2.00 pm – 5.00 pm Sundays. www.greatnorthmuseum.org 0191 222 6066

Housesteads Fort

6 miles east of Haltwhistle near the B6138, not far from Vindolanda.
Open daily 10.00 am – 6.00 pm, April to September; 10.00 am – 4.00 pm
October – March. Closed 24 – 26 December and 1 January.

Ravenglass Roman Bath House

East of Ravenglass, off a minor road leading to the A595.
Open daily all year round.
www.english-heritage.org.uk

Pike Hill Signal Tower

Near Banks village, north east of Brampton. Open daily.

Segedunum Fort, Wallsend

Open daily 10.00 am – 5.00 pm, April to October; 10.00 am – 3.00 pm November to March. Closed 25 – 26 December and 1 January. 0191 454 4093.

Senhouse Roman Museum, Maryport

Open daily 10.00 am – 5.00 pm, July – October; open Friday, Saturday, Sunday 10.30 am – 4.00 pm, November – March; open Friday, Saturday, Sunday, Tuesday, Thursday 10.00 am – 5.00 pm April-June. 01900 816168 www.senhousemuseum.co.uk

South Shields / Arbeia Fort

Open 10.00 am – 5.30 pm April – October, Monday – Saturday, 1.00 pm – 5.00 pm Sunday; 10.00 am – 3.30 pm November – March; 10.00 am – 3.30 pm Monday – Saturday closed Sunday. Closed 25 – 26 December and 1 January. 0191 456 1369.

Tullie House Museum, Carlisle

Open 10.00 am – 4.00 pm November – March, Monday – Saturday;
12.00 midday – 4.00 pm Sunday;
10.00 am – 5.00 pm April – June and September – October, Monday – Saturday;
12.00 pm – 5.00 pm Sunday;
10.00 am – 5.00 pm, July – August: Monday – Saturday, 11.00 am – 5.00 pm Sunday.
Closed 25 – 26 December and 1 January. 01228 534781 www.tulliehouse.co.uk

Vindolanda and Roman Army Museum (run by the Vindolanda Trust)

From the A69 take the B6318. Vindolanda is situated on a minor road near the village of
Bardon Mill. The Roman Army museum is a few miles to the west on the B6318.
Open daily from 10.00 am – 5.00 pm (6.00 pm April – September). A joint ticket can be
bought for access to both the site and the museum. www.vindolanda.com

Where to stay

Corbridge

Tourist Information Centre 01434 632815
Dilston Mill 01434 633493   www.visitnorthumberland.co.uk

Hexham

Tourist Information Centre 01434 65220
Langley Castle 01434 688888   www.langleycastle.com
West Close House 01434 603307

Housesteads

Twice Brewed Inn 01434 344534   www.twicebrewedinn.co.uk

Haltwhistle

Tourist Information Office 01434 322002
Centre of Britain 01434 322422   www.centre-of-britain.org.uk
Ashcroft 01434 320213   www.ashcroftguesthouse.co.uk

Greenhead

Holmhead Guest House 016977 47402   www.bandbhadrianswall.com

For general information

www.hadrians-wall.org

Opposite: The Royal Liver Building at Pier Head on the Liverpool waterfront.

Liverpool:
Maritime Mercantile City

Once a World Port; Now a City of Culture

Date of Inscription 2004

Why is it a World Heritage Site?

In the 18th and 19th centuries Liverpool was of pivotal importance to the British economy and to the growth of the British Empire because of its dominant position in global maritime trade. The city helped develop many innovatory technologies in dock construction and port management. Liverpool was a major centre for the slave trade until its abolition in 1807, and later became Britain's main port for mass emigration from Europe to America.

Location

The city is in north-western England, situated where the mouth of the River Mersey meets the Irish Sea.

HISTORY

The borough of Liverpool was founded in 1207 by letters patent of King John. The population had reached only 500 by the 16th century and it was not until 1699 that Liverpool was made a parish by Act of Parliament. This coincided with the first slave ship, *Liverpool Merchant*, setting sail for Africa.

The population had by this date been swelled by many London merchants who decided to leave the capital after the twin disasters of the Great Fire and the Great Plague. Celia Fiennes spoke of Liverpool in 1698 as a 'London in miniature' and of 'houses high and even' and people 'very well dressed and of good fashion'. Liverpool was also the port from where many religious emigrants, such as Quakers, left for the New World.

As the port expanded the Old Dock was opened in 1715. It became a prototype for a commercial enclosed wet dock and the catalyst for Liverpool's dominance as a world port. The main early imports were of tobacco, sugar and rum from the New World until the surge in the Triangular Trade (see box) involving the shipment of cotton, black slaves and other goods between Africa, the West Indies, America and Europe.

By 1801 a huge proportion of the world's trade was passing through Liverpool and it controlled 80 per cent of Britain's slave trade. The growth of canals in the

THE TRIANGULAR SLAVE TRADE

Liverpool was at the heart of the slave trade and much of its growth and prosperity was as a direct result of the profitable 'triangular trade'. Liverpool became pre-eminent in the trade because it had such good links by canal and river with the manufacturing centres of the north. The first element in the triangular trade was the shipment of goods that could be traded for slaves on the west coast of Africa, namely textiles from Lancashire and Yorkshire, copper and brass from Staffordshire and Cheshire, and guns from Birmingham.

From Africa the ships loaded slaves for the journey to the West Indies or the southern states of north America where they were sold – then sugar, rum and raw cotton were bought for the return leg to Liverpool. Georgian Liverpool itself had few African slaves except for individuals often sold by newspaper advertisement by ships' captains for use as 'fashionable' servants.

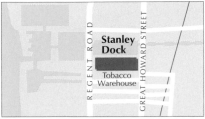

This above map is at the same scale as the main map, and is located on the River Mersey, approximately 500 metres further north

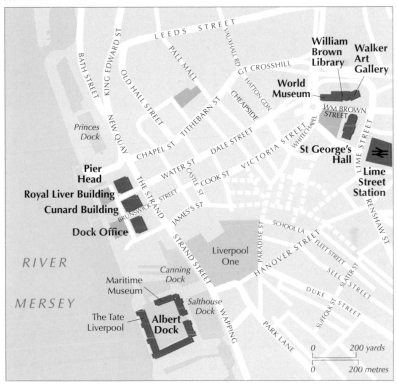

region during the 18th century, including a major link across the Pennines from Liverpool to Leeds, ensured that Liverpool played a pivotal role in the Industrial Revolution, the very substantial storage capacity in the docks being of crucial importance for cotton, iron and steel manufacturers. When the Liverpool to Manchester Railway was opened in the 1830s, a further link in the chain of efficient distribution of goods and people to and from the city's ports was completed.

As the town became more prosperous local industrialists and dignitaries wished to make it a place of culture and inspiration leading to the creation of the Cultural Quarter on St George's Plateau with its centrepiece, St George's Hall.

The strong lines of the Doric colonnade at Albert Dock, opened in 1846 by Prince Albert.

Six key areas are listed for the World Heritage site:

1. Pier Head with three main buildings – Royal Liver Building, the Cunard Building and Dock Office.

2. The Albert Dock Conservation area.

3. The Stanley Dock Conservation area to the north of Pier Head.

4. The historic centre to the east of Pier Head, around Castle Street, Dale Street and Old Hall Street with many outstanding buildings of the 18th and 19th centuries.

5. The Cultural Quarter including St George's Hall, the Walker Art Gallery, the World Museum and the William Brown Library.

6. Lower Duke Street, east of Stanley Dock with old warehouses and merchants' offices.

Key Locations

ALBERT DOCK

The dock was opened by Prince Albert in 1846 and includes the largest group of Grade I listed buildings in the UK. Beautifully restored, the harmony and solidity of the old buildings have now become a vibrant centre for a collection of museums, galleries, restaurants, cafes and shops. Located within Albert Dock are:

TATE LIVERPOOL

Tate Liverpool houses two main types of exhibits: displays from the Tate Collection and special exhibitions of modern and contemporary art. Twentieth and 21st-century pieces from the Tate Collection are shown in a series of themed displays which are changed regularly.

THE MERSEYSIDE MARITIME MUSEUM AND CUSTOMS AND EXCISE MUSEUM

Displays feature information about the growth of the port, its key role in World War II and the dangerous world of smuggling.

Jesse Hartley (1780–1860)

Jesse Hartley was the architect and builder of the Albert Dock. The son of an architect and bridgemaster from Yorkshire, he rose to become the highest paid engineer in the country. Every dock in the city was either built or altered by him at some stage. His vision for the docks was one of strength, mass and longevity. The Albert Dock 'is the unquestionable climax of Liverpool dock architecture' (Nikolaus Pevsner), constructed in granite blocks with five storeys and a splendid Doric colonnade. Hartley introduced many innovations to make dock buildings secure and fireproof notably by placing a layer of iron beneath timber floors and also using wrought-iron plates to produce a light but strong structure for the roofs. He also introduced locks to keep the water at a constant level so that loading and unloading ships' cargoes was not reliant on the tide. The docks all had high enclosing walls to deter thieves.

THE INTERNATIONAL SLAVERY MUSEUM

The museum's exhibits provide a thought-provoking analysis of the slave trade, the issues of reparation, racism and cultural change.

PIER HEAD

The iconic view of the Liverpool shoreline from the Mersey is dominated by the Royal Liver Building, the Cunard Building and the Mersey Docks and Harbour Board Offices – known collectively as the Three Graces. Together they seem to embody the grandeur and might of the British Empire.

ROYAL LIVER BUILDING

Built in 1908–10 by W. Aubrey Thomas the Royal Liver Building is an early example of reinforced concrete construction. Its eight storeys are surmounted by a central clock tower and two lower domes from which the legendary Liver Birds survey the Mersey and the city. (See photograph on page 175.)

THE CUNARD BUILDING

Begun in 1913, this was also constructed from reinforced concrete. Although less showy than its neighbours it has fine proportions and many neo-Grecian details with handsome lamps and other decorative details. The Cunard Building, headquarters of the Cunard Shipping Company until the 1960s, is noted in Liverpool for its distinctive shape being wider at the back than the front. It is said to have been designed like this to resemble a ship, widening from prow to stern.

MASS EMIGRATION

Liverpool was the primary European emigration port for America. Between 1830 and 1930 over nine million people sailed from Liverpool. Many emigrants from Scandinavia, Russia and Poland would cross the North Sea to Hull and then go by train to Liverpool. Irish emigrants came by steamship, especially during the potato famine of 1846–7.

Many emigrants spent up to ten days in Liverpool waiting to board their ship which gave ample opportunity for the local villains to fleece them in lodging houses which were often dirty and overcrowded. In the 1860s the situation improved when steamship companies such as Cunard agreed to take emigrants and looked after them during their stay in lodging houses run and owned by the company.

The South Portico of St George's Hall with the dramatic statue of Major General Earle astride the shield of a fallen African enemy. Born in Liverpool, he fought in most of the major battles in the Crimea and was killed at the Battle of Kirkeban in 1885.

MERSEY DOCKS AND HARBOUR BOARD OFFICES

This grand building in the classical style was erected in 1907 featuring a façade of 11 bays with three steep pediments and a large central copper-covered dome.

THE CULTURAL QUARTER

After the abolition of the slave trade in 1807, defended to the last by the Corporation, a new spirit was abroad in Liverpool which then became a prime mover in the campaign to abolish slavery entirely within the British colonies – finally achieved in 1833. The city then looked to reposition itself as a metropolis for the modern age aspiring to be a centre not only for commerce but for culture and cosmopolitan civilisation. The monumental classical buildings around William Brown Street are one of the best such groupings in the country.

St George's Hall

The hall was built between 1841 and 1854 by the architects Harvey Lonsdale Elms and C.R. Cockerell both as a concert hall and as a law court. The building is considered to be one of the finest examples of the Neo-Grecian style in the world. Its Great Hall, North Hall and Small Concert Room are magnificently decorated, featuring chandeliers and stained glass windows. The Great Hall has a historic Willis Organ and a tunnel vault inspired by the Baths of Caracella in Rome.

The Walker Art Gallery

The gallery was built with funds given by Sir Andrew Walker. The building is a handsome neo-Grecian edifice with Corinthian columns. The collection has grown over time as a result of further gifts from Liverpool families of money and works of art. The superb collection is now rich in European Old Masters (especially the early Italian and Netherlandish schools) and is also particularly strong in Pre-Raphaelite and later 19th-century British painting.

A street lamp outside St George's Hall.

The World Museum

The collections here have a wide scope. They cover natural and physical sciences, ancient history and archaeology. There are special exhibitions and permanent attractions such as the Clore Natural History Centre and the Bug House.

Lime Street Station

A wonderful Victorian railway station built 1867–1879 with a roof span of 61 metres (200ft), the largest in the world at the time of construction. It was built as the grand terminus for the Liverpool and Manchester railway, replacing two earlier railway sheds.

VISITOR INFORMATION

HOW TO GET THERE

By rail: There are regular services from London and all parts of the north west.
0845 485950 www.thetrainline.co.uk

By coach: National Express operate regular services from most major towns in Britain to Norton Street Coach Station 08705 808080 www.nationalexpress.com

By car: Motorway access from the M6 via the M58 or M62 or M56. Follow the brown roadsigns to the Waterfront or Central Tourist Attractions.

By air: Liverpool. John Lennon Airport
0151 907 1057 www.liverpooljohnlennonairport.com

TATE LIVERPOOL
0151 702 7400 www.tate.org.uk/liverpool

September – May
Open Tuesday – Sunday, 10.00 am – 5.50 pm
Closed Mondays (except Bank Holiday Mondays)
Closed on Good Friday, 24–26 December and 1 January

June – August
Open daily Monday–Sunday 10.00 am – 5.50 pm

THE MERSEYSIDE MARITIME MUSEUM AND CUSTOMS AND EXCISE MUSEUM
Open daily 10.00 am – 5.00 pm
0151 478 4499 www.merseysidemaritimemuseum.org.uk

THE INTERNATIONAL SLAVERY MUSEUM
Open daily 10.00 am – 5.00 pm
0151 478 4499 www.internationalslaverymuseum.org.uk

ST GEORGE'S HALL
Open daily (closed Mondays) 10.00 am – 5.00 pm
0151 233 2459 www.civichalls.liverpool.gov.uk

WALKER ART GALLERY
Open daily 10.00 am – 5.00 pm
0151 478 4199 www.thewalker.org.uk

THE WORLD MUSEUM
Open daily 10.00 am – 5.00 pm
0151 478 4393 www.worldmuseumliverpool.org.uk

WHERE TO STAY

General information: Tourist Information Centre
0151 233 2008 www.liverpool08.com

To book hotels in Liverpool and surrounding area:
Liverpool Accommodation Service 0844 870 0123

Radisson SAS Hotel
0151 966 1500 www.liverpool.radissonsas.com

Premier Inn, Albert Dock
0870 990 6434 www.premiertravelinn.com

Hope Street Hotel
0151 709 3000 www.hopestreethotel.co.uk

Salt's Mill seen from the Leeds and Liverpool Canal

Saltaire

*A Model Industrial Village and Testament to
Victorian Philanthropy*

Date of Inscription 2001

Why is this a World Heritage Site?

The mill village and settlement of Saltaire represent the high point of Victorian industrial philanthropy and follow in the footsteps of the Derwent Valley (see pages 117-123) and Robert Owen's New Lanark (see pages 225-232).

The 19th-century buildings are well preserved and the original lay-out and architecture survive intact. The harmonious, well-proportioned buildings reflect the inspiration of the village's extraordinary founder, Titus Salt, to create a model village where mill workers would be treated with respect, well housed and furnished with every modern amenity for themselves and their families. The factory itself was built using the most advanced technology of the age and the textile business flourished because it made intelligent use of an integrated transport system, namely the Leeds and Liverpool Canal and the Midland Railway.

Location

Saltaire is in West Yorkshire just 4 miles (6 kms) north west of Bradford.

HISTORY

By the mid-19th century Britain was experiencing an industrial boom and Bradford was one of the principal centres for the textile trade. The workforce had expanded from 8,500 in 1780 to 104,000 in 1850. The town's air was polluted, the workforce exploited and life expectancy dropped for both men and women to little over 20 years. The two waterways that ran through the town were like open sewers and the river was called the 'River Stink'. Families were crowded into inadequate living spaces sleeping four or five to a bed and smallpox and TB were ever present. Wool sorters were often exposed to anthrax when sorting fleeces from overseas, particularly Russian imports where the disease was endemic.

In 1825 the Woolcombers staged a strike in Bradford over pay and conditions that lasted over six months. It was only starvation that drove them back to the mills on the mill owners' terms.

Titus Salt became the mayor of Bradford in 1848. He attempted to solve the town's pollution and other problems but a cholera epidemic later that year proved to be a turning point and he decided to move his profitable business away from the town. He bought land a few miles from the centre of Bradford on the River Aire and named the new venture Saltaire. Work on the mill began in 1851. Bradford's leading architects Henry Lockwood and William Mawson worked in tandem with the engineer William Fairbairn whose job was to make sure that every possible structural and mechanical innovation was included in the final design.

As soon as the mill was up and running in 1853 work began on housing and

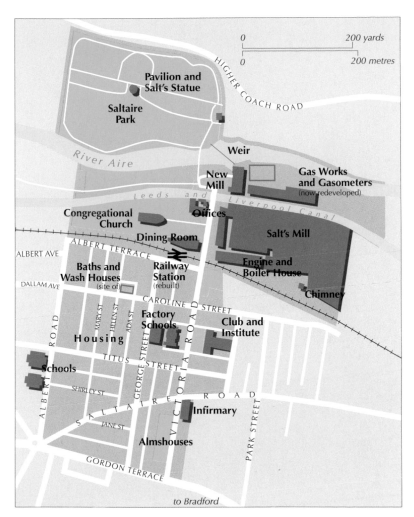

other amenities for the workforce who at first came from Bradford by train. The village eventually comprised over 800 houses set in wide streets with a large dining hall, baths and wash-houses, almshouses for the retired, a hospital, a school and church. Allotments and land set aside for recreation and sport together with facilities for swimming and boating on the river made Saltaire a model village in all aspects.

SALT'S MILL

The opening ceremony was held on Titus Salt's 50th birthday, 20 September 1853, and included a banquet for his 3,000 workers in the mill's combing shed.

Key Buildings

The *Illustrated London News* described it as 'probably the biggest dinner party ever set down under one roof at one time'. The feast consisted of fine meats and poultry followed by plum puddings, jellies, grapes, melons, peaches, pineapples and

This statue of Sir Titus Salt in Saltaire Park, with the tower of the church rising in the background, shows an angora goat on the base. The angora fleece produces mohair, the basis of Salt's commercial success.

nectarines. A band played during the meal and at 6 pm trains took the partygoers back to Bradford for a concert.

A huge building (which was served by a branch railway line) was built entirely of stone with an iron and brick interior to minimise the risk of conflagration. It is about 150 metres (nearly 500 ft) long and six storeys high. Its monolithic façade is broken up with some Italianate trimmings, turrets and towers. The roof structure gained its strength from cast-iron struts and wrought-iron rods allowing the space beneath the roof to be free of supporting piers – a huge empty space. The mill chimney at the eastern end is 68 metres high (220 ft).

The building was powered by two beam engines with 10 underground boilers.

The drive shafts and machinery were located underground to avoid the risk of injury and a subterranean reservoir supplied partly by rainwater was used for the engines and boilers.

The mill's output and scale of production were wonders of their time. The 1200 looms could produce 18 miles of worsted cloth in one day.

New Mill

On the north side of the canal the New Mill opened in 1868 and housed a spinning mill and dyeworks. Later work in the early 1900s added to the original single building and the complex now consists of two four-storey blocks between which rises an ornate chimney based on the campanile of a church in Venice, the Santa Maria Gloriosa dei Frari.

The church was erected in 1858-9 .

The Dining Room

As its name suggests this was where the workforce ate – 600 breakfasts and 700 dinners daily. It also doubled as a public meeting hall and schoolroom and was once linked by an underground tunnel to the mill. Above the central doorway is the Salt coat of arms.

The Congregational (now United Reformed) Church

This was built in 1858–9. The tunnel vault of the aisleless interior is supported by giant Corinthian columns and the interior is adorned with dark blue plaster work with a richly decorative coffered ceiling. The oak pews can seat a congregation of 600. A bust of Sir Titus Salt by Thomas Milnes was presented to him by his workers. The plinth is supported by an alpaca and an angora goat, the wools from which helped to make Sir Titus' fortune. He and his family are buried in the church's mausoleum.

*'From Peru, he has brought the
alpaca,*
From Asia's plains the mohair;
*With skill has wrought both into
beauty,*
*Prized much by the wealthy and
fair,*
*He has Velvets, and Camlets, and
Lustres;*
*With them there is none can
compare;*
Then off with your bonnets,
*And hurrah for the Lord of
Saltaire.'*

From a contemporary song about Titus Salt

ALMSHOUSES

These form a U-shape around Alexandra Square. There were once 46 houses each with oven, boiler and a single bedroom.

HOSPITAL

This has been extended since its first inception when it had only nine beds. The frontage on Saltaire Road has a central bay with a tympanum decorated with foliage and the Salt coat of arms.

SCHOOL

The school housed up to 750 pupils. It is a single-storey building comprising three pedimented pavilions linked by a tower and a three-bay open colonnade and features an elaborate bell turret with carved figures of a boy and a girl and a globe.

TITUS SALT (1803–76)

Titus Salt was born in Morley near to Leeds and brought up in a Nonconformist household. His father gave him a Bible with the inscription

' May this best volume ever lie,
 close to thy heart and near thine eye;
 Till life's last hour thy soul engage,
 and be thy chosen heritage.'

Later, as a father himself, Titus would present each of his 11 children with a pocket bible and write the same lines in each, just as his own father had done.

His father moved the family to Bradford in 1822 where he began a woolstapling business – trading and buying wool. Titus learnt all the skills of the wool trade – sorting, combing, spinning and weaving – in the Bradford firm of Rouse and Son but in 1824 joined forces with his father. The business took off when Titus made a success of spinning Donskoi wool from Russia and Peruvian alpaca wool which produced a lustrous, warm but light cloth ideal for women's fashionable dresses. Titus operated a cartel whereby he purchased all the imports of alpaca and, in due course, he opened an office in Peru, communicating with its staff in cipher.

After despairing of helping to improve living and working conditions in Bradford he bought the land that was to become Saltaire and built the huge Salt Mill in 1853 and the model village that was to grow up around it under his direction. He was made a baronet by Queen Victoria and at his funeral in 1877 it is said that over 100,000 people lined the streets of the funeral route to see his cortège.

INSTITUTE

Features a rich baroque entrance and a tower with a truncated spire. Originally it had a lecture theatre for 800 plus a smaller hall, a reading room, games room, billiard room, gym and kitchen.

HOUSING

The houses were built between 1854 and 1868 and each was equipped with its own water and gas supply and an outside lavatory. Most have yards at the back but a few more commodious houses were built with gardens for managers and white-collar workers. The town was built on a grid system and each house has a parlour and two or three bedrooms. Between the monotonous terraces were service lanes. Rents varied from three shillings (15 pence) to 5 shillings (25 pence) a week depending on the size of the house.

SALTAIRE REBORN TODAY

After Titus Salt's death the firm was run by three of his sons, its profits declined and it was wound up in 1892. Businessmen from Bradford revived its fortunes and after a boom in the interwar years of the 20th century the mills finally closed for good in 1986. Many of the buildings decayed until Jonathan Silver bought the complex in 1987 and turned it into a vibrant cultural centre with art galleries, (featuring in particular the largest collection of art by Bradford-born David Hockney), workshops and cafés.

An example of the solid housing built by Titus Salt for his workers.

Visitor Information

Opening Times

Open daily except for Christmas Day, Boxing Day and New Year's Day.

Monday – Friday 10.00 am – 5.30 pm: Saturday and Sunday 10.00 am – 6.00 pm
www.saltairevillage.info

Book a guided tour via the website or telephone 01274 599887 mobile 07952745471.

How to get there

By road: Saltaire is 4 miles north of Bradford and is 15 minutes drive from the M606.

By train: The Saltaire train station is opposite the mill and services connect to Leeds and Bradford.

Where to Stay

Great Victoria Hotel, Bradford 01274 728706 www.tomahawkhotels.co.uk

Lister Mansion Hotel, Bradford 01274 495827 www.listermansion.co.uk

Ponden House B & B, nr. Haworth 01535 644154 www.pondenhouse.co.uk

Opposite: The picturesque remains of Fountains Abbey in the remote valley of the River Skell.

Studley Royal Park including the Ruins of Fountains Abbey

A Majestic Ruin set in a Romantic Landscape

Date of Inscription 1986

Why is this a World Heritage Site?

An outstanding site due to its spectacular fusion of different natural and man-made elements, Fountains Abbey, the largest medieval ruin in the United Kingdom, is set within a great 18th-century garden in the valley of the River Skell enhanced by the natural backdrop of wild forest. In addition the late Elizabethan mansion, Fountains Hall, and the 19th-century church of St Mary's are both exceptional examples of buildings from their respective periods.

Location

The site is in North Yorkshire, four miles west of Ripon and 12 miles north of Harrogate. It is situated off the B6265. In the summer there is a shuttle bus from Ripon.

Fountains Abbey

The abbey was founded in 1132 by a group of dissident Benedictine monks from York. The archbishop of York directed them to Skelldale, 'a place remote from all the world'. A year or so later the monks decided to live by the ascetic rule of the Cistercian Order founded thirty years previously in Burgundy.

The new foundation was named St Mary of Fountains. Cistercian abbeys were always dedicated to the Virgin Mary but 'Fountains' may refer to the many springs in the valley or to the Order's inspiring guiding spirit, Bernard de Fontaines usually referred to as St Bernard of Clairvaux. The rules of the Order stipulated that monks wore a habit of coarse sheep's wool and led a spiritual life. This striving for simplicity was reflected in Cistercian architecture which avoided profuse decoration but achieved an austere splendour derived from the symmetry of the buildings, their mass and their wild settings. The monks were allowed to employ lay people to work for them, look after their flocks of sheep and help with other enterprises that (together with a number of important benefactions) brought the foundation great wealth.

The lay brethren had their own quarters within the monastery. They did not follow the strict monastic regime of prayer and contemplation, being permitted

---

THE DISSOLUTION OF THE MONASTERIES

Henry VIII (1509–47) was responsible for severing England's links with Rome and with papal authority. After his marriage to Anne Boleyn he was excommunicated; Parliament then passed the Act of Supremacy in 1534 which declared the king to be the Supreme Head of the Church of England. In 1539 Henry proceeded to abolish the entire monastic system in order to break the power of the Church and to fill his treasury. In 1536 there were over 800 monasteries, abbeys, nunneries and friaries that were home to over 10,000 monks and nuns. Fountains Abbey, which was the richest abbey in the kingdom, was dissolved along with countless other establishments. The lands were sold, the inhabitants expelled (although some were given pensions), and precious books and treasures lost or looted. Glass and lead from Fountains Abbey Church were taken to Ripon and York and stone used for the building of Fountains Hall.

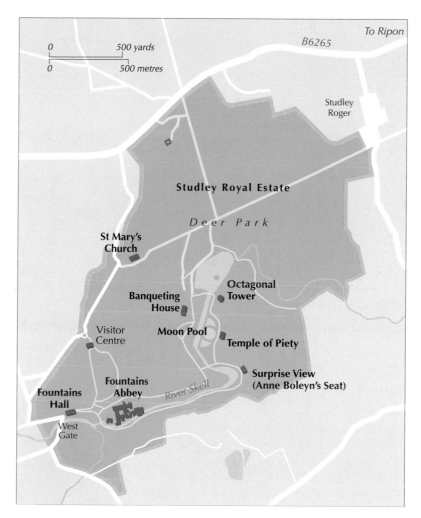

to sleep for longer, spending less time at mass and receiving a more generous diet than the monks.

Fountains' prosperity can be appreciated from the massive scale of the ruins – the abbey became the largest monastic building in Britain. Construction took place between the 12th and 16th centuries, continuing even through a period of mismanagement which precipitated a financial crisis in the 13th century. The roofless church and its 50 metre high (170 ft) tower – built by the last abbot – still stand together with a host of other monastic buildings such as the cloisters, chapter house, guest house, infirmary and remains of the abbey's mill, bakery and malt house, all erected along the river which provided water for washing, cooking, brewing and sanitation. The ruins provide an unrivalled snapshot of how a Cistercian community was organised.

The life of the abbey came to a sudden end when Henry VIII ordered the Dissolution of the Monasteries in 1539. The land was sold by the Crown to the

'Oh what a beauty and perfection of ruin!'
The Hon. John Byng

merchant Sir Richard Gresham and was then bought by Stephen Proctor who built Fountains Hall between 1598 and 1604 using some of the stone from the abbey ruins.

STUDLEY ROYAL PARK AND WATER GARDEN

The Studley Royal Estate was inherited by John Aislabie in 1693. Aislabie was a Yorkshireman who had risen to become Chancellor of the Exchequer but his brilliant career ended after the South Sea Bubble scandal and he was expelled from Parliament in 1721. Thereafter all his energies were directed towards the creation of the Water Garden and, although at that time, he did not own the abbey ruins, they were a key part of his scheme, providing the gardens with awe-inspiring viewpoints. Aislabie had little professional help for his vision apart from advice from Colen Campbell, the Palladian architect. All the works were carried out by local labour under the direction of the gardener, William Fisher.

In creating this beautiful garden John Aislabie used the river as its axis and made

maximum use of all the natural elements in the valley. Excavations were carried out on a huge scale to dig out and form the lake and ponds, the river was canalised, a dam and weirs constructed, and the valley floor levelled. Over a hundred labourers were needed to carry out the scheme – new trees were planted, many evergreen so the gardens would always have winter colour.

John's son, William Aislabie, continued the work on the garden. He was able to purchase the abbey remains and land for £18,000 and extended the landscaped area in the romantic manner of the day, a departure from the more formal geometric style of his father's time. The rough fields in the valley were turfed and the whole decorated with an assortment of temples and follies. These form dramatic contrasts with the valley's verdant layers of oak, lime and beech and with the exposed rock faces.

Temples, Follies and Statues
The Moon Pool (see below) has a statue of Neptune in the middle and is flanked by two crescent ponds and elegant statues of Bacchus and Endymion. Reflected in its water is the impressive Temple of Piety, Tuscan in style with a six-column

The Temple of Piety reflected in the Moon Pool – part of the romantic Studley Royal Water Gardens.

portico in golden stone. High on the cliff above, reached through a tunnel, is the Gothick Octagonal Tower with pointed arches and pinnacles, first built in 1738. Nearby are the remains of Aislabie's Kitchen, a spot where grand picnics were prepared for guests to eat at the Octagonal Tower. Southwards from this on the cliff is the rotunda, the Temple of Fame with classical detail. It looks as if it is made of stone but is in fact hollow timber with a simulated finish. The culmination

Above: The Banqueting House built in the 1730s.
Below: The Temple of Fame perched among trees on a low ridge overlooking the Moon Pool.

of William's grand ideas is seen in the Surprise View – from Anne Boleyn's Seat – where suddenly the trees and hedges open up to show a spectacular view of the ruins of Fountains Abbey. The structure once had sliding doors which would have added to the effect.

The Banqueting House was probably designed by Colen Campbell and was first planned in 1732 as an Orangery but its use was later changed. Originally the coffin lawn in front was surrounded by a clipped yew hedge.

The elegant East Gate with its central arched carriageway has another 'surprise view' as the towers of the Minster at Ripon are framed in the gateway as the

The rich and colourful interior of St Mary's church.

visitor leaves. It is no wonder that these gardens became one of the essential sights for the 18th-century traveller.

FOUNTAINS HALL

Completed in the first years of the 17th century for Sir Stephen Proctor, Collector of Fines on Penal Statutes, its stone came partly from the ruins of the abbey. Its style is influenced by the Elizabethan architect Robert Smythson, responsible for Hardwick Hall in Derbyshire and Burton Agnes in Yorkshire. In the 18th century the Hall was sold to the Aislabie family but as they lived in Studley Royal House (burnt down in 1946), the Hall was leased to tenants and much neglected. Fountains Hall underwent extensive repairs in the 20th century and is one of the National Trust's major restoration projects.

ST MARY'S CHURCH

An outstanding example of High Victorian Architecture by one of the masters of that style, William Burges. This church was built between 1871–78 for the Marquis and Marchioness of Ripon as a memorial to Frederick Gratham Vyner, Lady Ripon's brother, who had been murdered by Greek bandits in 1870. The money gathered to pay his ransom had not been spent and this was used to fund the building work.

> *'St Mary is the ecclesiastical masterpiece of William Burges, one of the most original and yet most characteristic of High Victorian architects.'*
>
> **Nikolaus Pevsner**

The church has a distinctive spire decorated with pinnacles and spirelets. Inside it is full of colour and gilding with lustrous stained glass, a vision of an idealised medieval world. The chancel arch has seven shafts on either side of black, red and green marble. The whole impression is one of glorious richness.

Visitor Information

How to get there

By road

The site is situated 4 miles west of Ripon and 12 miles north of Harrogate, off the B6265.

By public transport

There is a bus link to Fountains Abbey from Ripon. The Ripon Roweller bus service runs to Fountains Abbey three times a day, Mondays to Saturdays, and eight times a day on summer Sundays (May to September). Also on summer Sundays there are through bus services to Fountains Abbey on Dalesbus Fountains Flyer route 802 from Leeds, Otley and Pateley Bridge, and on Dalesbus Fountains Flyer route 812 from York, Boroughbridge and Ripon.

For details of all buses to Fountains Abbey: Traveline on 0870 608 2 608, or visit the Dalesbus website at www.dalesbus.org

To reach Fountains Abbey from Ripon it is also possible to take a taxi from the Market Square, or to walk (approx 4 miles each way).

Ripon has no railway station, but there are good bus links to Ripon from the railway stations at York (approx hourly on weekday daytimes) and Harrogate/Leeds (every 20 minutes on weekday daytimes, half hourly on Sunday daytimes and hourly during the evening). For details of train times call 08457 48 49 50 or see www.nationalrail.co.uk/planmyjourney/

By air

The nearest airport is Leeds Bradford International Airport (0113 250 9696). A daily bus link operates from the airport to Harrogate.

Opening times

Abbey and gardens

1 March – 31 October 10.00 am – 5.00 pm daily
1 November – 28 February 10.00 am – 4.00 pm open daily apart from Fridays in November, December and January. Closed on 24 and 25 December.
www.nationaltrust.co.uk

St Mary's Church

April – September 10.00 am – 4.00 pm

Places to Stay

To contact the nearest Tourist Information Centres:
Ripon TIC - 01765 604625   Harrogate TIC - 01423 537300

The National Trust has holiday cottages to rent on the Fountains estate and in Fountains Hall: www.nationaltrustcottages.co.uk

Best Western Ripon Spa Hotel 01765 602172 www.bw-riponspahotel.co.uk

Unicorn Hotel 01765 602202 www.unicorn-hotel.co.uk

Lawrence House B & B 01765 600947 www.lawrence-house.co.uk

Scotland

Old and New Towns of Edinburgh

Frontiers of the Roman Empire:
The Antonine Wall

New Lanark

Heart of Neolithic Orkney

St Kilda

Opposite: Edinburgh Old Town and the spire of The Hub seen from Princes Street Gardens.

Old and New Towns of Edinburgh

Scotland's Beautiful Capital

Date of Inscription 1995

Why is this a World Heritage Site?

Edinburgh has been the capital of Scotland since the 15th century. The two distinct central areas of the Old Town, dominated by its medieval castle and the New Town which was developed from the 18th century onwards, now form a harmonious whole. Each has many distinctive and important buildings but together they form a city with a unique character.

Location

Edinburgh is situated in the central lowlands of Scotland on the south shore of the Firth of Forth. It has a resident population of just under half a million but attracts over 13 million visitors a year and is the second most popular city for tourists in the United Kingdom after London.

HISTORY

In 1437 Edinburgh replaced Scone as the capital of Scotland. It had been a stronghold for local tribes since the Iron Age and excavations at Edinburgh Castle have found evidence of late Bronze Age settlements from *c.*850 BC. In AD 400 a tribe called the Votadini settled in 'Din Eidin' – the Fort of Eidin – and two hundred years later a poem describes warriors feasting 'in Eidin's Great Hall'. When southern Scotland became part of the northern kingdom of the Angles, known as Bernicia in the seventh century, the city was referred to as Edin-burh. In the 14th century the name settled into its current form, by which time the city had spread along the ridge between the castle and the abbey of Holyrood and 300 years later the inhabitants of the Old Town were still crammed onto this strip of land living in cramped, tall tenements.

As the population grew, the New Town was developed across the ravine which is now occupied by Princes Street Gardens and station. Wealthy denizens quickly made the transition from tenement to elegant Georgian house as the new suburb burgeoned into a magnificent assemblage of graceful, wide streets and spacious

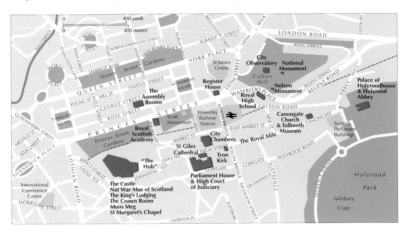

squares all locked into a neo-classical grid. However, the Old Town remained the hub for the legal, religious and academic life of the city (the university had been founded in 1583). The New Town attracted banking and insurance companies.

During the 19th century the population continued to grow and as the city swallowed surrounding farming communities new industries such as paper making, printing, mining and tanning flourished. The improvement of the port at Leith and the arrival of the railways in the second quarter of the 19th century gave further impetus to industrialisation. By 1951 the population of Edinburgh had reached nearly half a million.

The city has been the seat of the Scottish Parliament since its medieval origins and today has a new Parliament building commissioned after Devolution in 1998.

A view of the new Scottish Parliament building.

THE OLD TOWN

The Old Town, dominated by Edinburgh Castle strategically **Key Sites** positioned at the highest point of the volcanic crag, still retains its medieval lay-out. Anchored by the huge fortress at one end the Royal Mile sweeps down the ridge to Holyrood. Minor streets and narrow alleys (known as closes or wynds) branch downhill off the spine of the main road. As the 'V-shape' of the town narrows, early buildings thrust upwards to 10 or even 14 storeys. To make space many streets have vaults underneath, adding to the density of the Old Town.

The town was originally walled but the wall and the city suffered under the English invasion of 1544 and most of the earlier buildings seen today were constructed after this date. Building controls from the 16th century onwards enforced the construction of all roofs and façades using stone or slate to avoid the hazard of fire.

EDINBURGH CASTLE

The castle is open to the public but it is still a military headquarters for the British army, housing the HQ of the 52nd Infantry Brigade, the Royal Regiment of Scotland and the Royal Scots Dragoon Guards. There are two military museums within the castle walls. In front of the castle the sloping forecourt is known as the Esplanade where the famous Edinburgh Military Tattoo takes place each year. From here can be seen the Half Moon Battery, a round building which was erected

Edinburgh Castle seen from Princes Street.

in 1574 on the site of the ruined St David's Tower. The castle is entered through a gatehouse in front of the Battery.

THE KING'S LODGING

These date from the 15th century and are former royal apartments. They include the birth chamber where James VI of Scotland (James I of England) was born to Mary, Queen of Scots.

EDINBURGH CASTLE TIMELINE

*c.*3000 BC	Iron Age Hill fort
850 BC	Bronze Age settlement
AD 400	Known as the Fort of Eidin
*c*1070	First documented use as a castle during the reign of Malcolm III
1093	Queen Margaret dies after hearing the news that her husband Malcolm III had been killed at Alnwick
1296	King Edward I of England invades Scotland and captures the castle
1314	Sir Thomas Randolph, nephew of Robert the Bruce, climbs the north face of the castle rock and wins the castle back from the English garrison
1386	The three-storey David's Tower is built
1566	Mary, Queen of Scots gives birth to James VI in the castle
1568	Mary flees to England and James becomes king of Scots. The castle comes under siege from the king's supporters in what was known as the 'Lang Siege'
1573	David's Tower and other medieval walls shatter under bombardment
1688	The governor, who has declared for the Catholic James II, surrenders the castle to the English Crown
1707	England and Scotland are united and the Crown, Sword and Sceptre are returned to the castle
1996	The Stone of Scone is returned to the castle

THE GREAT HALL

Built during the reign of King James IV in 1511. An impressive structure with a hammerbeam roof it was used for meetings of the Parliament of Scotland before the construction of Parliament Hall in 1639.

THE CROWN ROOM

A vaulted chamber which contains the Honours of Scotland – the magnificent Crown jewels and regalia. The Scottish gold crown dates from 1540 and is set with 94 pearls, 10 diamonds and 33 other precious and semi-precious stones. Here one can also see the historic Stone of Scone, or Stone of Destiny, which was returned to Scotland from Westminster Abbey in 1996 (although it will travel to England for future coronations). Edward I, 'the Hammer of the Scots', removed it to London from Scone in 1296 (see p 96, Westminster Abbey).

NATIONAL WAR MUSEUM OF SCOTLAND

A museum that explains Scottish military history and contains many artefacts, uniforms and weapons.

MONS MEG

An enormous 15th-century siege gun that was later used for ceremonial purposes. It was made in Mons (in modern Belgium) and shipped to Scotland as a present for James II and his queen, Mary of Gueldres, and was last used in 1681 when, during a birthday salute to the Duke of Albany, the barrel burst. She weighs over 6 tons and can fire a stone shot of 150 kg (330 lbs).

ST MARGARET'S CHAPEL

This tiny chapel is the oldest building within the castle, dating from the early 12th century. It was built by King David I as a private chapel for the royal family and dedicated to his mother, Queen Margaret, who died in 1093 and was canonised in 1250.

PALACE OF HOLYROODHOUSE AND HOLYROOD ABBEY
HOLYROOD ABBEY

It was David I who founded the palace and the abbey. According to legend the king was attacked by a stag while out hunting one day; however, a silver cloud appeared in the sky above and a holy cross – or 'rood' – descended from it causing the stag to flee. In gratitude for his escape the king founded an Augustinian monastery in 1128 on the very spot of the miracle. The monastery grew into an abbey and many Scottish monarchs were married and buried there.

In 1544 it was pillaged by the Earl of Hertford and in 1688 plundered by a mob celebrating the accession of William of Orange who broke into the royal tombs. Despite restoration work carried out during the 18th century, the roof gave way and today all one can see are the evocative ruins north of the palace.

Medieval arcading at the remains of Holyrood Abbey.

PALACE OF HOLYROODHOUSE

At the end of the Royal Mile the palace was and still is a royal residence. The queen and other members of the royal family stay here while carrying out engagements in Scotland.

James IV (1488–1513) began the building of the palace as a residence for him and his new bride Margaret Tudor, the sister of Henry VIII. Only a trace of this original building survives today. His successor James V (1513–42) erected a large tower and a new west front with large windows to make it more suitable for domestic use. His second wife, Mary of Guise, was crowned in the abbey and their daughter, Mary, Queen of Scots (1542–67) would spend much of her turbulent life in the palace.

Mary married her two Scottish husbands in the palace and also witnessed the brutal murder of her private secretary Rizzio in her private apartments. These rooms are one of the highlights of a visit to Holyrood. They feature many display cabinets with a unique and sometimes poignant collection of Stuart relics. There is a brass plaque in a corner showing where Rizzio lay bleeding to death with over 50 dagger stab wounds. After her abdication the palace fell into decline and during the Civil War suffered further damage when English Parliamentary troops were billeted there. It was Charles II who was to come to the rescue and begin substantial rebuilding. He added a new royal apartment to the east, made the abbey church into a royal chapel and created spacious rooms on the second floor for the court when the sovereign was in residence.

Queen Victoria reintroduced the custom of staying at Holyroodhouse and it became once again Scotland's prime royal residence. In the 20th century George V and Queen Mary restored and updated the building, installing bathrooms and electricity and they began the custom of holding summer garden parties. This tradition has been upheld by Elizabeth II, and each year, she and the Duke of Edinburgh entertain around 8,000 guests from Scotland during Holyrood week.

Mary, Queen of Scots

1542	Born at Linlithgow Palace. Her father, King James V, dies six days later
1543	Mary is crowned Queen of Scots. The Earl of Arran is appointed Regent
1547	Betrothed to the dauphin of France, Francis, eldest son of Henri II and Catherine de Medici
1548	Mary is sent to the French court at the age of six
1554	Mary of Guise, (Mary's mother) is named Regent of Scotland
1558	At the age of 15 Mary marries the dauphin. Mary Tudor dies and Elizabeth I ascends to the English throne
1559	King Henri II of France dies and Francis and Mary are crowned king and queen of France
1560	Mary of Guise dies as does Francis leaving Mary without her mother and husband
1561	Mary returns to Scotland as a Catholic queen in a Protestant country with French as her first language
1565	Marries her 19-year-old cousin, Lord Darnley, in a Catholic ceremony
1566	David Rizzio, Mary's secretary, is viciously murdered by a jealous Lord Darnley in Mary's private rooms in Holyrood palace. Mary gives birth in Edinburgh Castle to the future James VI of Scotland
1567	Lord Darnley is murdered. Mary and the Earl of Bothwell are suspected of murder. In May Mary and Bothwell are married in the Council Hall of Holyrood – whether Mary was coerced by Bothwell or was willing has never been established. A revolt ensues, Mary is imprisoned in Lochleven castle and abdicates. Her infant son is crowned king of Scotland
1568	Mary flees to England where she is imprisoned
1586	Tried for conspiring against Elizabeth I
1587	Mary is executed in the Great Hall of Fotheringay Castle in Northamptonshire
1603	King James VI also becomes James I of England on Elizabeth's death. He moves his mother's body to Westminster Abbey

The Royal Mile

One Scottish mile long, the Royal Mile runs between Edinburgh Castle and down to Holyrood Abbey. The streets which make up the Royal Mile are, from west to east, Castle Esplanade, Lawnmarket, High Street, Canongate and Abbey Strand. It is rich with important and interesting buildings, churches and other historical attractions.

'The largest, longest, finest street in the world.'

Daniel Defoe on the Royal Mile

Scottish Parliament

The striking new Parliament building is opposite Holyroodhouse and overlooked by the dramatic natural landscape of Salisbury Crags and Arthur's Seat. Its construction began in 1999 and it was formally opened in September 2004 by the queen. The architect, Enric Miralles, drew his inspiration from the natural setting as well as the work of Charles Rennie Mackintosh and upturned boats. It is made of steel, oak and granite and won the 2005 Stirling Prize for architecture.

Canongate Church on the Royal Mile.

CANONGATE CHURCH
Designed by James Smith and completed in 1691 this church has a sinuous curved outline. Neatly proportioned, it features a large central window crowned with the royal arms of William of Orange.

CANONGATE TOLBOOTH
With its turreted steeple this is the oldest remaining building in Canongate. It was where tolls and taxes were collected and was built in 1591 in the French style of the time. Below it was the gaol. The prominent clock is a 19th-century addition.

TRON KIRK
The striking 19th-century steeple of this church is an addition to the original 17th-century church situated on the junction of the Royal Mile and South Bridge. No longer used as a place of worship it is now an exhibition centre.

THE CITY CHAMBERS
Set back from the High Street, this building houses the town council and was built to the neoclassical designs of Robert and James Adam in 1753.

ST GILES CATHEDRAL – THE HIGH KIRK
St Giles' was founded in the 12th century and is a mixture of medieval Gothic and early Renaissance architecture. The

The High Kirk seen from the east.

RIOT AND CIVIL WAR

In July 1637 St Giles witnessed the first incendiary incident in a chain of events which had the most profound consequences not only for Scotland but also for the other kingdoms within the British Isles. King Charles I of Scotland and England, in an effort to impose a form of Anglican observance on Scotland (which since the Reformation had become, in the most part, increasingly strongly Presbyterian), required that the Book of Common Prayer be used in Scottish churches. When the dean of St Giles began to read from this book a riot ensued, sparked, it is said, when a woman by the name of Jenny Geddes threw a stool at the dean. This event lead to the formation of the National Covenant which sought to preserve Presbyterianism and oppose the interference of Charles in Scottish religious affairs. The king responded in 1639 by launching a catastrophically mismanaged invasion of Scotland, known as the first Bishop's War, which ended in ignominious failure. A second Bishop's War in 1640 ended in further shameful dishonour for the English. This conflict between England and Scotland led directly to the outbreak of prolonged Civil War in the three kingdoms of England, Scotland and Ireland, the eventual victory of the Parliamentary army in England, the execution of Charles I in January 1649, the abolition of the monarchy and the establishment of the Commonwealth under the leadership of Oliver Cromwell.

beautiful crown spire was added in the 1400s. Unfortunately the building was unsympathetically 'restored' in the 19th century but the interior is still full of interest, notably the early 20th-century Thistle chapel with an abundance of detailed carving. This chapel is the spiritual home of the The Most Ancient and Most Noble Order of the Thistle, Scotland's premier order of chivalry, founded by James VII (James II of England) in 1687. Elsewhere there is a striking statue to John Knox, Victorian stained glass and a splendid memorial to Robert Louis Stevenson.

THE PARLIAMENT HOUSE AND HIGH COURT OF JUSTICIARY

This is located just off the Royal Mile adjacent to St Giles Cathedral and was the home of the Scottish Parliament until union with England in 1707. The oldest part of the building is Parliament Hall built during the reign of Charles I and features a superb arched oak roof spanning 15 metres (50 ft). It is now used for the Court of Sessions and other courts of law. In the 1800s the architect Robert Reid added a new façade and open arcades to the building.

THE HIGHLAND TOLBOOTH ST JOHN'S CHURCH – 'THE HUB'

This former church on Castlehill is now the administrative centre for the Edinburgh International Festival and is nicknamed 'The

The Hub seen from the Esplanade.

Charlotte Square in the Georgian New Town.

Hub'. The original neo-Gothic church dates from 1844 and is the work of James Gillespie Graham and Augustus Pugin who was responsible for the landmark 73 metre (240 ft) spire which is the highest point in the city centre.

THE NEW TOWN

The New Town of Edinburgh is without doubt one of the finest examples of planned 18th-century architecture in the world with a high concentration of neoclassical buildings all to a consistent style. What makes Edinburgh so important is that so much of the original scheme has survived intact with the notable exception of Princes Street where very few 18th-century buildings remain.

The New Town was envisaged as a residential area for the nobility and the merchant classes. An architectural competition in 1766 was won by the 22-year-old

James Craig who planned a grid of five streets centred on George Street, occupying the top of the ridge which runs parallel to the old town, intersected by a further seven streets. Charlotte Square completes the scheme at the west end with St Andrew Square at the east. Work started in 1767. In 1801–2 the plan was extended by Robert Reid and William Sibbald and included some curved terraces. Later two more architects, William Henry Playfair and James Gillespie Graham, began to use the natural contours of the land, its trees and views to set off the buildings.

Although the original idea was that the New Town should be solely residential it soon proved to be attractive to business and government and became the location for some of the best public and commercial urban development in the classical revival style. The planned ensembles are what make the New Town special but a few of the more famous buildings are detailed below.

THE REGISTER HOUSE

Robert Adam, together with his brothers James and John, designed this monumental building, which houses the National Archives of Scotland. Built between 1774 and 1792 it faces the North Bridge axis contributing to one of Edinburgh's many great formal vistas.

THE ASSEMBLY ROOMS

Fashionable Edinburgh society was keen to follow in the footsteps of Bath and have a splendid Assembly Rooms of its own. In 1783 the foundation stone was laid in George Street. John Henderson had won the competition for his design but he died halfway through its construction and his son, David, continued his work. It opened – in an unfinished state – in 1787 and the elegant and well-proportioned rooms were further embellished with wonderful chandeliers, Corinthian pilasters and opulent mirrors over the next fifty years or so.

The Assembly Rooms have seen many distinguished historical events such as George IV's visit in 1822 (painted by Turner), a public banquet in honour of Charles Dickens and a Commonwealth Heads of Government Meeting in 1997.

NATIONAL GALLERY AND ROYAL SCOTTISH ACADEMY

These two institutions are situated right in the heart of Edinburgh on the Mound. The Royal Scottish Academy was designed by William Henry Playfair; work started in 1822. The adjacent National Gallery of Scotland was Playfair's last project, begun in 1851. These two neoclassical buildings, positioned as they are on this salient point between the 'gothic' Old Town and the Classical New Town, form a perfect link between the two. Their graceful proportions have helped to give Edinburgh the reputation of being the 'Athens of the North'.

THE MOUND

The Mound is a man-made bluff formed by the dumping of vast quantities of spoil generated by the digging of foundations for the New Town and as a result of draining the Nor' Loch – now Princes Street Gardens. It provides a convenient crossing point between the Old and New Towns.

A raking view of the side elevation of William Henry Playfair's neoclassical National Gallery of Scotland.

THE ROYAL HIGH SCHOOL

Another exceptional example of neoclassical architecture, the school was designed by Thomas Hamilton in 1825. It is located on the southern edge of Calton Hill. The Doric columns on its frontage are based on the Temple of Theseus in Athens.

> *'Lord Nelson, as befits a sailor, gives his name to the top-gallant of the Calton Hill. This latter erection has been differently and yet, in both cases, aptly compared to a telescope and a butter-churn; comparisons apart, it ranks among the vilest of men's handiworks.'*
>
> **Robert Louis Stevenson**

CALTON HILL MONUMENTS

At the east end of Princes Street lies Calton Hill with its bizarre collection of buildings and monuments, among them the Nelson Monument built in 1807 which was an attempt to render Nelson's telescope in stone. A visit will be rewarded with wonderful panoramic views of the city, the Forth estuary and the Forth rail and road bridges. In 1852 a large 'time ball' was installed which drops at exactly 12 noon Greenwich Mean Time. Mariners were able to see this from Leith harbour and could set their marine chronometers against an exact time. During British Summer

Time the release of the Time Ball coincides with the firing of the one o'clock gun in Edinburgh castle.

The City Observatory of 1818 is also situated on top of the hill together with Observatory House designed by James Craig in 1776. Nearby is the Playfair Monument and the National Monument which was designed by Playfair and C. R. Cockerell (who modelled it on the Parthenon) to commemorate the fallen of the Napoleonic wars. It seems that it was never completed due to lack of money – only 12 columns were erected – but it may have been the case that it was always intended as a romantic folly.

Once again Athens proved the inspiration for another Playfair building on the hill – the monument to the philosopher Dugald Stewart erected in 1831 which is modelled on the Choragic Monument by Lysicrates.

On the eastern side of the hill is the castellated Governors House, all that remains of the huge Calton gaol which was replaced by the art deco St Andrew's House – now the administrative home of the Scottish government.

Visitor Information

Opening Times

Edinburgh Castle

Open all year seven days a week:
1 April to 31 October 9.30 am – 6.00 pm
1 November to 31 March 9.30 am – 5.00 pm
Closed 25 and 26 December
0131 225 9846

Palace of Holyroodhouse and Abbey

Open daily: 1 April – 31 October 9.30 am – 6 pm
1 November – 31 March 9.30 am – 4.30 pm
Closed 25 and 26 December and during Royal visits.
0131 556 5100 www.royalcollection.org.uk

Scottish Parliament

Business days (normally Tuesday – Thursday): all year 9.00 am – 6.30 pm
Non-business days (normally Mondays and Fridays and every weekday when Parliament is in recess) April to September 10.00 am – 5.30 pm; October to March 10.00 am – 4.00 pm
Saturdays and public holidays: all year 11.00 am – 5.30 pm; Closed Sundays.
Visitor Services for advice on visiting the Parliament on 0131 348 5200;
email sp.bookings@scottish.parliament.uk.

National Galleries Complex and Royal Scottish Academy

Open daily 9.30 am – 5.00 pm (until 7.00 pm on Thursdays)
0131 225 6671 nginfo@nationalgalleries.org

The Nelson Monument, Calton Hill

April – September: Monday 1.00 – 6.00 pm; Tuesday – Saturday 10.00 am – 6.00 pm
October – March: Monday – Saturday 10.00 am – 3.00 pm

How to get there

By road: Scotland's capital is well served by road links : AI, M74 then M8, M90.

By air: Edinburgh International Airport receives direct flights from a wide range of destinations across Europe, North America and elsewhere in the UK.

By sea: ferries from Rosyth port, less than an hour away from Edinburgh, provide daily services to the Continent via Zeebrugge.

By train: Waverley Station is in the heart of the city centre. High-speed inter-city train services along Britain's East Coast mainline link Edinburgh to major centres throughout eastern England as far as London while the West Coast mainline connects the city with areas such as the Lake District, Chester and Bath.
National Rail Enquiries: 08457 484950 From abroad: 44 (0) 20 7278 5240
www.nationalrail.co.uk

All of Edinburgh's access points boast excellent bus, taxi or rail facilities linking them with the city centre.

www.visitscotland.com/library/travellingtoedinburgh

Where to Stay

General information

The Tourist Information Centre in Princes Street can book accommodation for a small booking fee: 0845 2255121 Email: info@visitscotland.com
www.edinburgh.org/accom

The Witchery Apartments 0131 225 5613 www.thewitchery.com

Balmoral 0131 556 2414 www.roccofortehotels.com

Six Mary's Place Guesthouse 0131 332 8965 www.sixmarysplace.co.uk

Opposite: An aerial view showing traces of the Antonine Wall.

Frontiers of the Roman Empire: The Antonine Wall

Rome's Short-lived Boundary in Caledonia

Date of Inscription 2008

Why is this a World Heritage Site?

The Antonine Wall is part of the transnational site 'Frontiers of the Roman Empire' which includes the remains of Roman frontier fortifications in the British Isles and Germany; it was built about twenty years after Hadrian's Wall (see pages 163-174) from AD 142. Its adoption is due to international co-operation to ensure the preservation of the Roman borders in Europe. The Antonine Wall was the northernmost frontier of the Roman Empire and bears witness to the various, sometimes troubled, attempts of the Romans to subdue Scotland.

Location

The wall is 37 miles (60 km) long and runs between Carriden on the Firth of Forth to Old Kilpatrick on the Firth of Clyde.

HISTORY

The first concerted attempts by the Romans to conquer Scotland came under the leadership of the governor of Britain, Agricola, after about AD 80. In a number of campaigns he built roads and forts – including some on the narrow Forth-Clyde isthmus. Agricola's strategy was to force the dominant tribes of Caledonia (the Roman name for Scotland) to a pitched battle in order to break their resistance. This event took place at Mons Graupius in AD 83 or 84 where the Caledonian tribes under the leadership of Calgacus were routed. According to the Roman historian Tacitus, 10,000 Scottish warriors died, but as Tacitus was Agricola's son-in-law this number should be treated with considerable caution. However, it is clear that the northern tribes were no match for the disciplined Roman army. Following this victory, Agricola was recalled to Rome and shortly afterwards the army abandoned its most northerly forts, withdrawing to the Tyne-Solway line soon after AD 100.

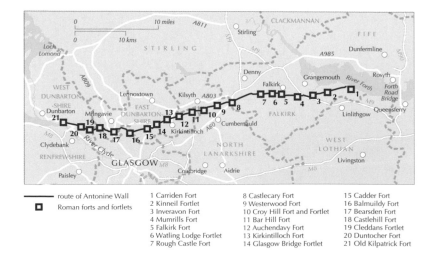

—— route of Antonine Wall	1 Carriden Fort	8 Castlecary Fort	15 Cadder Fort
▢ Roman forts and fortlets	2 Kinneil Fortlet	9 Westerwood Fort	16 Balmuildy Fort
	3 Inveravon Fort	10 Croy Hill Fort and Fortlet	17 Bearsden Fort
	4 Mumrills Fort	11 Bar Hill Fort	18 Castlehill Fort
	5 Falkirk Fort	12 Auchendavy Fort	19 Cleddans Fortlet
	6 Watling Lodge Fortlet	13 Kirkintilloch Fort	20 Duntocher Fort
	7 Rough Castle Fort	14 Glasgow Bridge Fortlet	21 Old Kilpatrick Fort

Here Hadrian's Wall was constructed in the years following 122 in order to define the limits of the empire. It served to control access to the province while the troops based along its line protected the local inhabitants from attack.

It was Hadrian's successor as emperor, Antoninus Pius, who once more instructed the governor of Britain, Quintus Lollius Urbicus, to push the Roman frontier further into Caledonia and it was this line of fortifications that became known as the Antonine Wall. Construction was completed in about three years but about twenty years later, after Antoninus' death, the line was abandoned.

Britannia during Antoninus' reign was regarded by some as an economic burden within the empire, its conquest seen more as a mark of glory than of practical use to Rome. Historians now believe that Antoninus Pius ordered the advance north and the construction of the Antonine Wall in order to bolster his position on the throne. It is interesting that no attempt was made to complete the conquest of the island at this time and although the Romans had some notable victories against the tribes they never truly conquered Caledonia and indeed the two walls with their forts and defensive structures are a testament to their failure to do so. They were ultimately defeated by the hostility of the native population, the terrain and the heavy demands on their resources. As one of the emperor's officials, the Greek Appian, noted:

'The Romans have aimed to preserve their empire by the exercise of prudence rather than to extend their sway indefinitely over poverty-stricken and profitless tribes of barbarians.'

EMPEROR ANTONINUS PIUS (AD 86–161)

Titus Aurelius Fulvus Boionius Arrius Antoninus Pius succeeded Hadrian as emperor of Rome, ruling between 138–161. Hadrian had adopted him as his son and successor. One of Antoninus' first acts as emperor was to persuade the Senate to deify Hadrian (about which they had been reluctant); it was probably this that gained him the title of 'Pius' meaning 'dutiful in affection'. His reign was one of relative peace, prosperity and financial prudence (at his death he left a surplus of 675 million *denarii*). All this appears to have resulted in him being a popular emperor – at least this is the impression given by the few contemporary sources.

Unlike other emperors it seems that he never left Italy during his long reign and delegated military problems to his provincial governors. So, after the emperor made the decision to build the wall that now bears his name, the execution of the order was entirely in the hands of his local governor. It was possible that Antoninus wanted to emulate his illustrious predecessor's example in erecting a wall, but no doubt he was also responding to news of unrest in Caledonia and the continuing incursions of its unruly inhabitants.

Antoninus' famous successor Marcus Aurelius paid this tribute to him: 'Remember his qualities, so that when your last hour comes your conscience may be as clear as his.'

HOW THE ANTONINE WALL WAS BUILT

It is estimated that it would have taken about 7,000 men to build the Wall which originally stood about 4 metres (13 ft) high and was constructed of turf blocks resting on a stone foundation. It may have been topped with a palisade of sharpened wooden pikes. On the north side a large V-shaped ditch about 12 metres (40 ft) wide and 4 metres (12 ft) deep provided extra protection. Alongside the south side there was a cobbled road used for transporting materials, known as the 'Military Way'. The road linked a network of forts and fortlets built at roughly two-mile intervals along its length.

Distance Slab now at the Hunterian Museum in Glasgow.

WHAT TO SEE TODAY

Many parts of the Wall are no longer visible, lost in farmland or beneath towns and other settlements but substantial parts of it still remain and can be seen today. The eastern terminus of the wall was the Carriden Fort by the Firth of Forth near to Bo'ness but no trace of this is visible.

KINNEIL FORTLET AND MUSEUM

The first place of significance is the Kinneil Fortlet on the Kinneil Estate near Bo'ness where there is also an exhibition of artifacts from the Antonine Wall in the

Kinneil museum; exhibits include Roman coins, brooches, sandals and a harness. Excavations in 1978 showed that the fortlet was situated to the rear of the Wall with a gravel road running north to south through the fort. Timber posts now mark the positions of the original Roman buildings.

POLMONTILL

From Kinneil the Wall made its way west on a high ridge past Inveravon Camps and Fort but it is only at Polmontill (near the present-day ski slope) that a short section of the ditch can be seen. Midway between this and Callendar Park is where the largest fortification on the wall once stood – Mumrills Fort. Now there is just a large and empty ridge but archaeological excavations have discovered a little about the life and times of the soldiers who once served there. Extensive remains of animal bones from chickens, oxen, deer, pigs and sheep were found alongside oyster and whelk shells. Ceramic cheese squeezers were discovered, showing that the garrison even made their own cheeses, and fragments of amphorae from the Mediterranean that once contained both sour and sweet wines, speak of some consolations for the troops on this lonely stretch of the Wall. A tombstone to one of the soldiers records his name, age, length of service and origin: 'Nectovelius, son of Vindex, aged 29, of 9 years service, a Brigantian by tribe'. It is interesting that he was a native Briton – the Brigantes were a tribe occupying what is now northern England – happy to serve as a Roman soldier.

CALLENDAR PARK AND MUSEUM, FALKIRK

Running westwards from the Business Park is a clear view of the Antonine Wall ditch in the grounds of Callendar Park. Over a length of about half a mile it is about 2–3 metres (6–10 ft) deep. The only sign of the wall itself is a low mound set back from the southern end of the ditch between two lines of trees.

The Wall continued through the present-day town of Falkirk.

WATLING LODGE, TAMFOURHILL

This location affords the most impressive view of the ditch that flanked the wall. It is some 12 metres (40 ft) wide and 5 metres (16 ft) deep and shows what a formidable barrier it would have been.

ROUGH CASTLE FORT, NEAR BONNYBRIDGE

Although this was a relatively small fort (which would have accommodated about 200 soldiers) it is the best preserved fortification on the Wall. It was built against the rear of the Wall protected by 6 metre (20 ft) thick turf ramparts with double ditches surrounding the other three sides. The wall today is about 1.5 metres (about 5 ft) high and the ditch and rampart are in good condition.

Over the causeway and across the great ditch is a remarkable ancient Roman booby trap for any approaching enemy. A cluster of pits in the ground, known as *lilia*, remain. Each one would have had a sharp pointed stake at the bottom with brushwood on the top, to trap and impale anyone trying to get across to the fort.

Geoff Bailey, keeper of archaeology and local history at Falkirk Museum, writes:

The remains of the Wall at Rough Castle.

'We have now found these *lilia* on eight separate occasions and it looks like they will have gone along the whole 38 miles of the wall. They are another part of the defensive system which had never been discovered before. The Romans would have had the ditch, the wall and these *lilia*, which you could call the ancient Roman equivalent of the minefield.

'The Germans had similar structures called wolf pits in the First World War, and they were used relatively recently in the Vietnam war where they were smeared with animal fat, so that any injury inflicted would become infected.

'We just don't know if the Romans did something similar here, but they provided an extra obstacle for people moving north to south and channelled people into the heavily guarded gateways where they could be easily controlled.'

Near to the fort are the Bonnyside expansions which were turf platforms about 5 metres (16 ft) square, normally built in pairs and set by the inner rampart wall. It is thought they were used to send signals north and south of the Wall as the remains of fires have been found. Similar structures in the Roman world are shown on Trajan's Column in Rome.

SEABEGS WOOD

To the south of the Forth and Clyde Canal at Seabegs Wood the

Lilia at Rough Castle fort – '... the ancient Roman equivalent of the minefield ...'

Antonine wall and ditch can be easily seen for about a quarter of a mile through the wood. Two miles away is Castlecary Fort where excavations found evidence of Roman occupation from the time of Agricola right up to the Antonine period. Several altars were discovered dedicated to different gods and goddesses such as Mercury and Neptune, including one to Fortuna with the inscription: 'To Fortuna, the detachments from the Second Augustan Legion and the Sixth Victorius Legion, Loyal and faithful, gladly and freely place this.'

The line of the Wall continues west through further forts such as Westerwood Fort, Croy Hill and Bar Hill Fort, the highest of all forts along the wall with excellent views of the surrounding countryside. Inscriptions found at Bar Hill show that it was garrisoned by a crack unit from Syria famous for its archery skills – another example of the huge reach of the Roman Empire. The low mounds forming the defences of the fort are visible and inside the headquarters building and the bath-house have been excavated and laid open for inspection. Beside the Roman fort is a small Iron Age fortlet, Castlehill.

Auchendavy Fort was partly destroyed during the building of the Forth and Clyde Canal in the late 18th century when 'navvies' digging the canal unearthed a group of five Roman altars dedicated to a total of 11 gods, including 'the spirit that watches over Britain'. Kirkintilloch Fort lies within Peel Park, its name derived from the Celtic 'Caerpentaloch' which means fort at the head of the hillock. Nearing Glasgow the Wall's next landmarks are Glasgow Bridge Fortlet, Cadder Fort and Balmuildy Fort. In New Kilpatrick Cemetery, Bearsden, two lengths of the stone base of the Antonine Wall can be seen.

BEARSDEN BATH HOUSE

In suburban Glasgow, stones and foundations from the Bearsden Bath House and its latrine can be seen on the north side of the Roman road. A beautiful carved head to the goddess Fortuna was found during its excavation in 1973 and is now exhibited in the Hunterian Museum. At the west end of Bearsden, a short length of ditch and a section of Wall base can be inspected in Roman Park.

CASTLEHILL FORT

This overlooks Drumchapel, marked by a circle of beech trees and is about 120 metres (400 ft) above sea level which would have afforded the soldiers superb views north, east and westward over the Clyde estuary towards the coast. At the top of the hill the Wall alters its alignment from west to south west to cross the stream at the bottom and then turns west again to climb Hutcheson Hill to the site of the fortlet at Cleddans. A distance slab (see box on page 220) was found at Hutcheson Hill with the following inscription: 'For Imperator Caesar Titus Aelius Hadrianus Antoninus Augustus Pius, father of his country, a detachment of the Twentieth Legion Valiant and Victorious have made three [thousand] four-hundred and eleven paces [of the wall].'

Duntocher Fort sits on Golden Hill, its ramparts picked out by differential grass cutting. A short section of the Wall can be seen. Beside the Clyde the last fort, Old Kilpatrick Fort, has vanished under modern developments.

Visitor Information

Museums where finds and artefacts from the Antonine Wall are exhibited

Hunterian Museum, University of Glasgow, University Avenue, Glasgow

The museum holds finds from the western part of the Wall including most of the distance slabs and other artefacts such as the head of Fortuna from Bearsden.
Open Monday – Saturday 9.30 am – 5.00 pm.
0141 330 442 www.hunterian.gla.ac.uk

Museum of Scotland, Chambers Street, Edinburgh

Includes the Bridgeness Distance Slab and finds from the eastern part of the Wall.
Open daily 10.00 am – 5.00 pm.
0131 225 7534 www.nms.ac.uk

Kinneil Museum, Kinneil Estate, Bo'ness

Finds from Kinneil Fortlet which is a short walk from the museum.
Open Monday – Saturday 12.30 pm – 4.00 pm.
01506 778530 www.falkirk.gov.uk

Callendar House, Callendar Park, Falkirk

Presents a permanent exhibition on the Wall. Part of the structure can be seen in nearby Callendar Park.
Opens Monday – Saturday 10.00 am – 5.00 pm (Last admission 4.00 pm).
Sunday 2.00 pm – 5.00 pm (Last admission 4.00 pm).
01324 503772

Auld Kirk Museum, Cowgate, Kirkintilloch

Local material and finds from Bar Hill Fort.
Open Tuesday – Saturday 10.00 am – 1.00 pm and 2.00 pm – 5.00 pm.
0141 578 0144 www.eastdunbarton.gov.uk

How to Get There

By road

The eastern end of the wall, at Kinneil / Bo'ness can be reached from the M9, exit junction 4. Use the same motorway for Falkirk if approaching from the east or north, or the M876 from the west. For the central section use the A803 which runs to the north of the line of the wall. For Castlehill and Bearsden use the A810 and local roads.

By rail

The rail service between Glasgow and Edinburgh via Falkirk will enable the visitor to get fairly near to the wall. Alight at Linlithgow for Kinneil.

Where to Stay

Bishopton (near Old Kilpatrick Fort): The Millers House 01505 862417
www.themillershousebandb.com

Airth Castle (near Falkirk) 01324 831411 www.airthcastlehotel.com

Antonine Wall Cottages (Bonnybridge – Self-catering) 01324 811875
www.antoninewallcottages.co.uk

Opposite: The factory village of New Lanark on the fast-flowing River Clyde.

New Lanark

*A Progressive Utopia founded by
Robert Owen*

Date of Inscription 2000

Why is this a World Heritage Site?

It was here, in this steep wooded valley, that Robert Owen (see below) began a Utopian and philanthropic industrial community. The original cotton mills, the workers' housing, the school and educational institute all set up by Owen are still intact and the whole site is a testament to his humane and progressive thinking which challenged the exploitative systems prevalent in the cotton industry. The ethical practices at New Lanark had a profound influence on social developments throughout the 19th century in both Britain and Europe.

Location

The village of New Lanark is in southern Scotland close to the Falls of Clyde, less than an hour's drive from Edinburgh and Glasgow.

HISTORY

New Lanark was founded in 1785 by David Dale, a yarn merchant, and Richard Arkwright, the pioneer of industrial cotton-spinning. Arkwright saw the potential of harnessing the fast-flowing River Clyde to power the mills and believed the site had the potential to become the Manchester of Scotland.

The first mill began production in 1786 by which time Dale had become sole proprietor. Dale built three- and four-storey blocks of housing for his workers and also established a school. In 1793 there were 1,157 employees – 362 adults and almost 800 children from the ages of six upwards who often came from orphanages. Child labour was common in 18th-century Britain and by all accounts Dale looked after the children very well. They were housed in clean conditions in No. 4 mill, given a change of clothes and fed properly with porridge for breakfast and barley broth with 'good fresh beef' for dinner. However their working hours were long – from 6 in the morning until 7 at night after which they were meant to attend the school for two hours.

In 1799 Dale's daughter, Caroline, married Robert Owen, then 27 years old, who subsequently bought the four textile mills for £60,000.

Owen's Utopian vision was not altogether pleasing to his partners and it was not until many years later in 1814 that Owen was able to buy them out and find more sympathetic investors such as the forward-looking economist and philosopher, Jeremy Bentham, and the Quaker, William Allen. Owen could then start putting his innovative ideas into practice to try to create a community, now numbering over 2,000 people, which could flourish in a benevolent environment. He believed

'Of all the places that I have yet seen I should prefer this in which to try an experiment I have long contemplated and to have an opportunity to put into practice.'
Robert Owen's statement when he first viewed New Lanark

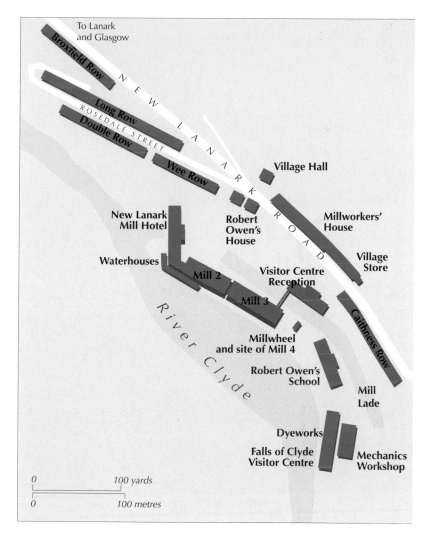

that if you treated your workers well their characters would be improved and that this, in turn, would lead to greater productivity.

When Owen arrived in New Lanark, children as young as five were still working 13 hours a day. He refused to employ children under the age of 10 and reduced working time to 10 hours a day. He built new nursery and primary schools for the youngest children and a secondary school for the older ones who attended lessons for part of the day. He also built a 'New Institution for the Formation of Character' to help educate his adult workforce with evening classes.

Owen abolished physical punishment in the factory and schools. All the villagers had free medical care, a sickness fund, a savings bank, and a village store that sold affordable food and household goods. At this time many factory owners gave tokens to their workers which could be exchanged only at company shops. The goods in these factory stores were often shoddy and expensive.

THE SILENT MONITOR

This was part of Owen's management system of his workers. Near to each worker's position a four-sided piece of wood was suspended. Each side had a different colour that showed the employee's performance as judged by the factory superintendents: Black – Bad, Blue – Indifferent, Yellow – Good, White – Excellent. This allowed Owen to see at a glance how each employee was working and deal with it without resorting to abuse or beatings as had been common practice.

New Lanark became a place of pilgrimage for social reformers, statesmen and even royalty including the future tsar, Nicholas, of Russia. The mills themselves flourished but Owen still had problems with his partners, eventually severing his connection with New Lanark in 1824 to found a community in Indiana.

New Lanark mills continued to spin cotton under new management until 1881 when the concern was sold to a partnership which added net-making and canvas weaving to their output as the cotton industry in Britain was in decline. The mills then passed to the Gourock Ropework Company producing canvas and net as well as rope until 1968 when the mills closed down with a loss of 350 jobs.

However, the site was regenerated in the 1970s with the founding of the New Lanark Conservation Trust which has pioneered a radical approach to heritage conservation and revitalised the community. Now over 400,000 visitors a year come to experience Robert Owen's vision of a new society set amongst the beautiful surroundings of the valley.

Key Sites

Walking around the narrow valley, always accompanied by the sound of rushing water, gives the visitor a powerful sense of how life would have been with a bustling community of workers and children in a relatively small space.

VISITOR CENTRE

This is housed in three of the village's historic buildings. Entry is via the aptly named Institute for the Formation of Character where one of the world's first infant schools began. In the adjoining Engine House there is a restored Petrie steam engine, and an introductory video on the story of New Lanark can be viewed.

In Mill Three the Millennium Experience Ride takes you back into the 1820s with the aid of a beguiling laser show. Downstairs is an example of a working 19th-century spinning mule and other textile machinery plus models of the factory, a copy of a 'Silent Monitor' and other informative exhibits.

ROBERT OWEN'S SCHOOL FOR CHILDREN

This recreates an 1820s New Lanark classroom with such innovative features as a Musician's Gallery and painted canvases on the walls which were used as teaching aids. The children wrote on slates and wore cotton uniforms.

ROBERT OWEN (1771–1858)

'It is therefore, the interest of all, that every one, from birth, should be well educated, physically and mentally, that society may be improved in its character, - that everyone should be beneficially employed, physically and mentally, that the greatest amount of wealth may be created, and knowledge attained, - that everyone should be placed in the midst of those external circumstances that will produce the greatest number of pleasurable sensations, through the longest life, that man may be made truly intelligent, moral and happy, and be thus prepared to enter upon the coming Millennium.' Robert Owen

Owen was a man ahead of his time and his work inspired infant education, humane working practices, the co-operative movement, trade unionism, and garden cities.

There were three guiding principles to his philosophy: first, that 'no one was responsible for his will and his own actions', that is he thought that people were the result of their environment and upbringing. This led him to think that children and adults could be favourably influenced by a good education and a decent environment. His second tenet was his anti-religious stance; he believed that religion made a person 'a weak, imbecile animal; a furious bigot and fanatic; or a miserable hypocrite'. Thirdly he disliked the factories and the power that machines were given; he preferred cottage industries and the subordination of machinery to the good of the workforce.

THE MILLWORKERS' HOUSE

Two recreated tenements, one from the 1820s and one from the 1930s, can be seen showing how people slept, washed and cooked. The rest of the building has been creatively restored into modern dwellings and house about 180 people.

THE VILLAGE STORE

In the far corner of the Village Square is the store that Robert Owen opened to help improve his workers' standard of living. This was the inspiration for the co-operative movement whereby goods were bought in bulk with a proportion of the resultant savings being passed on to members.

FACTORY REFORM

Robert Owen was a zealous supporter of factory reform and his ideas influenced the governments of the day in continuing to legislate to limit the exploitation of children.

- 1819 Factory Act: No children under 9 to work in factories. Children from 9 to 16 to work a maximum of 72 hours per week with one-and-a-half hours a day for meals.

- 1833 Althorp's Factory Act: Children from 9 to 13 to work a maximum of 42 hours a week; children from 13 to 16 to work a maximum of 69 hours a week. No night work for anyone under 18.

- 1842 Mines and Colliery Act: All women and children under 10 banned from working underground. No one under 15 to work winding gear in mines.

- 1844 Graham's Factory Act: Minimum age for working in factories reduced to 8 years old. Children between 8 to 13 years old to work a maximum of six-and-a-half hours a day. Between the ages of 13 to 18 the working day was capped at a maximum of 12 hours; this also applied to women. Safety guards to be fitted to all machines.

- 1847 Fielden's Factory Act: A 10-hour day introduced for under-18s and for women.

strong winds hit the islands. In the summer there is almost no darkness for about six weeks. The island scenery is very beautiful with numerous lochs and the grass meadows and cliff tops are a vivid green in contrast to the shimmering and everchanging seascape.

Maes Howe

The Maes Howe mound is just over 500 metres from the shore of the Harray loch and is visible for miles all around. The mound was constructed on a platform of levelled ground like the nearby stone circles of Brodgar and Stenness and was surrounded by a ditch and raised bank; it is possible that the encircling ditch was once a moat. Another theory suggests that the site once housed a stone circle. Before it was first excavated in 1861 its shape was conical with a depression in the top and it stood 11 metres (36 ft) high. In 1910 Maes Howe became the property of the state and a concrete roof was added.

This is the finest chambered tomb in north-west Europe. It lies beneath a mound 35 metres (114 ft) across and now only 7 metres (23 ft) high. A long passage of 11 metres (36 ft) lined with slabs of stone leads to a substantial chamber

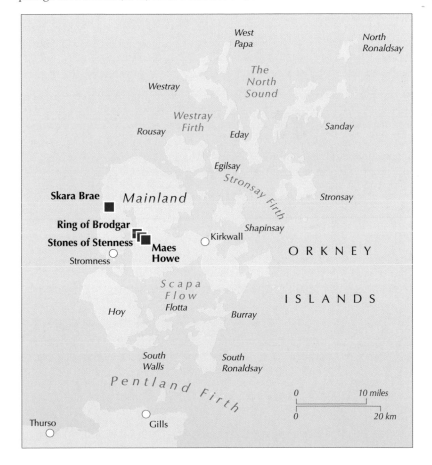

Maes Howe: the burial mound is visible for miles.

4.5 metres (15 ft) square; each corner is supported by a pillar. Recesses in the walls of the chamber held the remains of the dead.

Constructed with 30 tons of sandstone, Maes Howe is one of the largest tombs in Orkney – it is estimated that it would have taken 100,000 man hours to construct. The tomb is aligned so that as the midwinter sun slips below the horizon on the winter solstice its final rays shine through the entrance passage to light up the back wall of the central chamber. This awe-inspiring feat of engineering and applied astronomy is shared with the chambered tomb of Newgrange in Ireland (see pages 253-4).

Its entrance was sealed with a massive wedge of stone in *c.*1500 BC and it remained undisturbed until AD 1150 when Norse pirates who were spending the winter on the island broke into the tomb – possibly seeking shelter – and left runic inscriptions.

THE RUNES

According to the Orkneyinga Saga, Earl Rognvald of Orkney led his followers on a crusade to the Holy Land in 1150. On 6 January 1153, Harald Maddadarson landed in Orkney from Argyll in an effort to take the islands in the absence of the earl. He and his men broke into Maes Howe through the roof and spent some time sheltering there. Later in 1153 Earl Rognvald and his followers returned from their crusade, and they in turn explored the newly opened tomb.

The evidence for this comes directly from the walls of the tomb, which carry many examples of graffiti left by the Vikings in the form of carved runes. Examples include 'Ottarfila carved these runes'; 'Tholfr Klossienn's son carved these runes high up' (high on the wall near the roof); or the less modest 'These runes were carved by the man most skilled in runes in the western ocean with this axe owned by Gauk Trandilsson in the South land'; 'Thorni bedded, Helgi' carved on the wall of one of the side chambers: Thorni was a woman's name. Elsewhere, in the main chamber, 'Ingigerth is the most beautiful of women.' Other carvings include a beautifully drawn and carved animal which some take to be a lion or a dragon, a serpent or even a walrus.

The Stones of Stenness are over five thousand years old.

STONES OF STENNESS

These 12 thin slabs of standing stones were erected around 3,000 BC in the form of an ellipse enclosed by a ditch 6 metres (20 ft) wide and 2.3 metres (7 ft) deep. Now only four remain but their height, their extraordinary thinness and position still make this an inspiring site.

If the visitor stands within the centre of the circle and looks between the two dolmen stones with a large prone stone beside them, there is an alignment to the distinctive mound of Maes Howe. This might indicate that the stones formed some sort of symbolic link between the two sites.

The Watchstone is a monolith 5.5 metres (17 ft) tall at the south end of the causeway between the Lochs of Harray and Stenness. The nearby Odin Stone was destroyed by a farmer in 1814 but luckily he was stopped before more damage occurred.

RING OF BRODGAR

'[In Stenness] beside the lake are stones high and broad, in height equal to a spear, and in an equal circle of half a mile.' Jo Ben *c.*1529

This huge ceremonial enclosure is situated on high ground in the centre of a huge 'cauldron' formed by the surrounding hills, about a mile from the Stones of Stenness, on the Ness o' Brodgar, a narrow strip of land separating the Harray and Stenness lochs. The original 60 tall stones formed an exact circle of 104 metres (330

THE RING OF BRODGAR

The Ring of Brodgar was first recorded in an account of Orkney, *Descriptio Insularum Orchadiarum,* written by Jo Ben who may have been a travelling monk or priest in the 16th century. In 1792 the ring had 18 standing stones with eight lying on the ground. However, by 1815 there were only 16 left standing and in 1854 the position had deteriorated with only 13 erect stones, 10 complete, but fallen stones and fragments of 13 more. In 1906 the ring was taken into state care and by 1918 most of the fallen stones had been restored to what was thought to be their original places. Twenty-seven stand today after two suffered direct lightning strikes.

ft) in diameter surrounded by a large ditch and were originally sited at 6 degree intervals. It has two entrance causeways and with a diameter of 103.6 metres (340 ft) is the third largest stone circle in the British Isles (exactly the same size as Avebury's two inner rings). Unfortunately only 27 stones now remain, the second highest megalith having been shattered by lightning on 5 June 1980.

The ring may have been constructed to observe, record and possibly celebrate solar and lunar events – although there is no firm evidence that this was its

purpose. The date of its creation has been estimated at between 2,500 and 1,500 BC – probably the last of the great Neolithic structures built on the Ness. Some 13 burial mounds surround the ring, the most important of which, Salt Knowe, Plumcake Mound and South Mound, were built and used during the same period.

The area surrounding the World Heritage Site also has a number of funerary, ritual and domestic sites contemporary with stone circles, notably the Barnhouse Settlement with houses built of stone and turf with similar interiors to those at Skara Brae. A stone with carving similar to ones found in Skara Brae and Maes Howe was found in Barnhouse.

SKARA BRAE

On the southern shore of the curve of the lovely Bay of Skaill is the settlement of Skara Brae. It was not until a great storm of 1850 that this Neolithic village was laid bare – it had been buried beneath sand dunes for centuries. Because of this and because it is constructed of stone, not wood, it is in exceptionally good condition and offers a unique view into the lives of the people who built it and lived there some time between 3,000 and 2,500 BC.

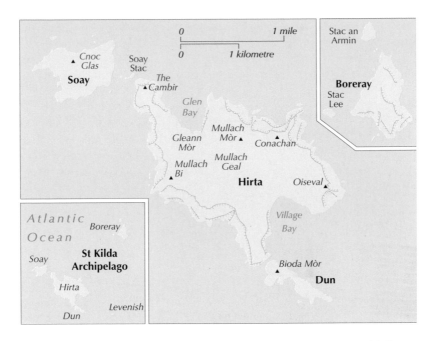

presence in settlements such as Oiseval, the east hill, and Ruaival, the red hill.

The population of St Kilda spoke Gaelic and probably never numbered more than 180 but the numbers slowly dwindled to just 36 inhabitants who were evacuated at their own request on 29 August 1930.

The only residents now are military personnel (St Kilda has been part of a missile tracking base since 1957) plus occasional conservators and volunteer work parties from the National Trust for Scotland and researchers.

For many centuries St Kilda was owned by the MacLeods of Harris and Dunvegan whose stewards would visit to collect rents which were paid in kind –

THE MISTRESS STONE RITUAL

'In the face of the rock, south from the town, is the famous stone, known by the name of the mistress-stone; it resembles a door exactly; and is in the very front of this rock, which is twenty or thirty fathom perpendicular in height, the figure of it being discernible about the distance of a mile; upon the lintel of this door, every bachelor-wooer is by an ancient custom obliged in honour to give a specimen of his affection for the love of his mistress, and it is thus; he is to stand on his left foot, having the one half of his sole over the rock, and then he draws the right foot further out to the left, and in this posture bowing, he puts both his fists further out to the right foot; and then after he has performed this, he has acquired no small reputation, being always after it accounted worthy of the finest mistress in the world: they firmly believe that this achievement is always attended with the desired success. This being the custom of the place, one of the inhabitants very gravely desired me to let him know the time limited by me for trying of this piece of gallantry before I design'd to leave the place, that he might attend me; I told him this performance would have a quite contrary effect upon me, by robbing me both of my life and mistress at the same moment.' *Martin Martin*

barley, oats, fish, birds and produce from the islanders' cattle and sheep rearing. The islanders appear to have been quite self-sufficient and St Kilda even had a reputation for abundance. A chaplain would accompany the steward to baptise children although it seems that the islanders' religious knowledge was very rudimentary.

View of the Main Street from above showing Cleits (top left) and Fanks.

CLEITS

Scattered all over St Kilda are the 'cleits' of which over 1200 remain on Hirta alone. They are small drystone constructions roofed with stone slabs which are then covered with earth and turf. The open walls allowed the fierce winds to flow through them without causing damage. They were used to store everything from birds, eggs, feathers and harvested crops, as well as peat which was used for fuel.

AGRICULTURE

Families had different plots scattered in the fertile ground and land was divided according to the traditional 'run-rig' system common elsewhere in Scotland. The ground was divided up into strips – or rigs – for arable use. The deep furrows allowed excess water to drain away. The remains of irregular sheep folds or 'fanks' lie behind Village Bay.

CATCHING BIRDS

Seabirds are ubiquitous on St Kilda and the islanders were incredibly skilful in catching them and harvesting their eggs by either lowering themselves in baskets to the ledges of the cliffs or otherwise climbing up often sheer rock faces to nests from the bottom. They took gannets, fulmars and puffins for food, feathers and

oil. The birds were caught either by hand, or with a snare or fowling rod. When Henry Brougham visited the island in 1799 he remarked that 'the air is infected by a stench almost insupportable – a compound of rotten fish, filth of all sorts and stinking sea-fowl.' The islanders rarely fished because of the heavy seas and treacherous and changeable weather.

THE ST KILDA PARLIAMENT

The men of St Kilda gathered every day in The Street to share news after morning prayers to plan what tasks they needed to undertake together – perhaps the rounding up of sheep or catching birds on the cliffs. No one led the meeting and all present had the right to speak. This meeting came to be known as the St Kilda Parliament.

THE OUTSIDE WORLD

Visiting ships were no doubt very welcome for their novelty value but often they brought disease to the islanders. In 1724 a smallpox epidemic killed many and new families came from Harris to fill the gap that was left by the deaths; however, the carefully balanced social structure of the island began to falter. From the 1870s St Kilda began to be visited by tourists and money was introduced into the economy for the first time. The islanders made cash from the sale of knitted goods, tweed and bird eggs but their traditions were perhaps eroded by these contacts.

RELIGION

It was unfortunate that the rich traditions of music and poetry on the island withered with the visit of a strict evangelical preacher, the Reverend John MacDonald in 1822. Known as the 'Apostle of the North' he believed in a strict puritanical church. In 1829 Neil MacKenzie became the resident minister.

The Church may have improved the islanders' lives with the foundation of a school and helping to rebuild village houses, but the strictness of the Reverend John MacKay who came in 1865 and his insistence that Sundays were spent in three lengthy services, each one lasting two to three hours, and his talk of hellfire and damnation for any who transgressed against his puritanical beliefs, no doubt dampened the spirits of the islanders and many of their essential routines were disrupted. One visitor to the islands noted that 'The Sabbath was a day of intolerable gloom.'

THE ST KILDA 'MAILBOAT'

If the islanders needed to communicate with the outside world they had to light a beacon on the summit of Conachair and pray it might be seen by a passing ship. However, in 1877 after a shipwreck on the islands, a certain John Sands sent a message out on a lifebuoy salvaged from the wreck which told of the plight of the marooned sailors. The message was picked up on the Orkneys and the sailors were rescued. The islanders then adapted the idea by carving a tiny boat (the St Kilda Mailboat) into which they would place a cocoa tin with a message and launch it when the winds came from the north west so that the tin would hopefully arrive in Scotland – although sometimes they strayed to Norway. A 'mailboat' from St Kilda carried greeting to the new Scottish Parliament in 1999 and took only a few weeks to arrive.

Remaining houses on 'The Street'.

The Village

Sixteen houses remain of the original 25 to 30 'black houses' as they were called. Each was made of dry stone and covered with turf; a typical dwelling had just one small window and an opening to let out the smoke from the peat fire that burnt in the middle of the room. Straw was laid on the floor and cattle would live in one end of the house in winter. The National Trust for Scotland have re-roofed some of the houses and modernised their interiors for use by working parties but have kept one close to its original state.

Military installations

In the First World War a signal station was constructed on Hirta by the Royal Navy and for the first time daily communication was possible with the outside world. Perhaps because of this Village Bay was attacked in May, 1918 by a German

The Evacuation

After the First World War many of the young men left St Kilda and the population fell from 73 in 1920 to 37 in 1928. The lack of medical care and any infrastructure led to four men dying of influenza in 1926 and then, after the tragic deaths of two young women in January 1930, the islanders determined that they could not sustain life on the island. On 29 August 1930 the last 36 people left St Kilda for the Scottish mainland never to return.

'The morning of the evacuation promised a perfect day. The sun rose out of a calm and sparkling sea and warmed the impressive cliffs of Oiseval… observing tradition the islanders left an open Bible and a small pile of oats in each house, locked all the doors and at 7 a.m. boarded *The Harebell*… they were reported to have stayed cheerful throughout the operation. But as the long antler of Dun fell back into the horizon and the familiar outline of the island grew faint, the severing of an ancient tie became a reality and the St Kildans gave way to tears'. From *Island on the Edge of the World: the Story of St Kilda* by Charles Maclean

submarine which fired 72 shells and destroyed the wireless station. Luckily the only casualty was a lamb. A naval gun was then erected on a promontory overlooking the Village Bay.

In the Second World War there was no protection given to the islands but they bear the scars of aircraft crashes and some of the wreckage still remains. In 1955 St Kilda became part of a missile tracking range based in Benbecula and in 1957 permanent inhabitants once again came to its wild shores. Since then a variety of military buildings and masts have gone up on land leased by the Ministry of Defence from the National Trust for Scotland.

> *'Whatever he studies, the future observer of St Kilda will be haunted the rest of his life by the place, and tantalised by the impossibility of describing it, to those who have not seen it.'* **James Fisher, naturalist**

THE NATURAL WORLD

In 1931 Lord Dumfries (later 5th Marquess of Bute) purchased the islands from Sir Reginald MacLeod. The marquess died in 1956 and bequeathed the archipelago to the National Trust for Scotland. In 1957 it was designated a National Nature Reserve. In 1986 it was inscribed as a World Heritage Site for its terrestrial natural features and in 2004 this recognition was extended to include its marine habitat which support an internationally important seabird colonies of over a million birds.

In 2005 St Kilda was inscribed as a cultural landscape that bears exceptional testimony to over two millennia of human occupation in extreme conditions.

St Kilda's geographical isolation has meant that there are unique species, including a mouse and a wren, on the archipelago and it is a prime example of a lack of biodiversity. The islands' fantastic landscape – itself a wonderful example of its volcanic origin – is a safe habitat for many rare and endangered species.

BIRDS

Of vital importance to birdlife, St Kilda has one of the largest concentrations of breeding populations in the North Atlantic. It boasts the largest colony of Northern gannets in the world – about a quarter of the world's stock. There are approximately 49,000 pairs of Leach's petrels (one of the very few places in Europe where they breed), 136,000 pairs of Atlantic Puffins

St Kilda is home to 136,000 pairs of Atlantic Puffins.

and 67,000 Northern Fulmar pairs. The Great skua or bonxie has been seen hunting petrels at night. In 1840 the last Great Auk to be seen in Britain was killed on Stac an Amin. A subspecies of the wren is unique to the islands, *Troglodytes troglodytes hirtensis*.

ANIMALS

Grey seals are to be found in the waters around the islands and after the evacuation in 1930 they returned to breed on Hirta. The St Kildans bred up to 2,000 Soay sheep, a very primitive breed that does not require shearing; there are now many left on Hirta and also a feral colony on Soay. There is also a St Kilda fieldmouse found only on these shores.

PLANT LIFE

The plants on the archipelago have again adapted to the conditions of high humidity, the peaty soil and the effect of salt spray plus the benefits of the fertilising droppings from the huge numbers of seabirds. Although there are no trees the islands support a full range of plants with over 130 species of flowering varieties.

VISITOR INFORMATION

HOW TO GET THERE

For full and up-to-date information visit www.kilda.org.uk and www.culturehebrides.org

There are a variety of ways to get to these remote islands. Charter Boats run from Mallaig and Oban on the Scottish mainland and from the Western Isles; touring companies also visit the islands. A journey on a motor boat from Oban will take up to 14 hours – even from the Western Isles it may take up to eight hours.

Visitors are welcome to travel to St Kilda by sea using their own transport, such as a private boat or yacht. It is helpful if independent travellers contact the Trust with details of intended travel plans, particularly details of landing and departure times.

National Trust for Scotland
Balnain House, 40 Huntly Street
Inverness IV3 5HR 01463 232 034

PLEASE NOTE THE FOLLOWING POINTS:

- The only accommodation on the island for visitors is a small campsite, which takes a maximum of six people and must be booked in advance. Campsite booking details and availability can be obtained from the above office.

- Dogs (and other domesticated animals) are not permitted on the islands.

- All visitors to the island should contact the Ranger on arrival. Please try to avoid visiting on Tuesdays and Fridays, as these are supply days.

WORK PARTIES

National Trust for Scotland work parties have been making the long sea journey to this island archipelago for over 50 years. The work parties take the form of a working holiday with members participating in essential conservation work; this may include repairing stone walls, turf roof repairs, clearing drains and repainting as well as helping with the day-to-day running of the island. Work parties normally visit between May and July.

For further information contact:

St Kilda Work Party Co-ordinator, National Trust for Scotland at the above address.

Ireland

Archaeological Ensemble of the Bend of the Boyne

Giant's Causeway and Causeway Coast

Skellig Michael

Opposite: Sunrise on the Winter Solstice illuminates the central passageway at Newgrange.

Archaeological Ensemble of the Bend of the Boyne

A Spectacular Ancient Ceremonial Site

Date of Inscription 1992

Why is this a World Heritage Site?

This is one of the most important prehistoric sites in Europe and also one of the best preserved. It is also cited because of the continuity of its use from the 4th millennia to the early 2nd millennia BC and then from the Early Iron Age to the High Middle Ages. On two counts therefore it is a storehouse of information about the social, economic and religious organisation of past cultures.

Location

The area of Brú na Bóinne covers some 780 ha (315 acres) and is, as the name suggests, on the River Boyne; the main locations are on a ridge running east-west with the three great mounds of Newgrange, Dowth and Knowth crowning the area surrounded by about 40 passage-graves, the whole making a huge prehistoric landscape.

The site is about 8 km (5 miles) inland from Drogheda in the County of Meath in the Republic of Ireland. It is 50 km (30 miles) north of Dublin.

HISTORY

There are traces of prehistoric man in Ireland before the great Neolithic monuments were constructed. Mesolithic remains exist of early Irish farmers who built isolated homes and many miles of stone boundaries presumably for their livestock or crops and also cleared ancient woodland. It is thought that a wave of invasions, perhaps from Brittany, heralded the New Stone Age with a population who were not

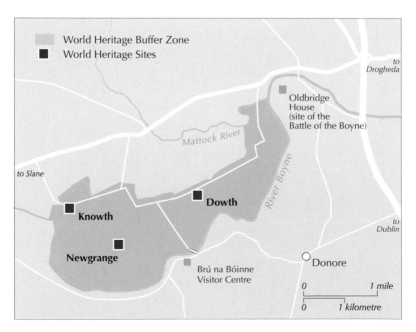

only farmers but builders on a grand scale. Apart from the ensemble at the River Boyne there are also three extensive 'cemeteries' – Carrowmore and Carrowkeep in County Sligo and Loughcrew in County Meath. However, these are all dwarfed by the necropolis at Brú na Bóinne.

After these Stone Age people came the Bronze Age Beaker folk who were, in turn, succeeded by Celts probably from about the first millennium BC. Indeed it was the Celts who named the area Brú na Bóinne meaning the dwelling place of the goddess Boyne. Celtic myths relate how she had an affair with the sun god Dagda and then gave birth to Aengus Óg, the god of youth and beauty who claimed the site for his own.

Later it was construed as a burial place for the mystical kings of Tara. During the medieval period it came under the control of the local Cistercian abbey at Mellifont who owned the land and incorporated it into their system of granges or estate farms, hence 'newgrange'.

THE VISITOR CENTRE

The Brú na Bóinne Visitor Centre is on the south side of the River Boyne and overlooks the sites. It was opened in 1997 and is the starting point for all visitors wishing to visit Newgrange and Knowth. A shuttle bus service runs to the monuments from the centre. There is no direct access to the monuments except by guided tour.

There is also a permanent exhibition explaining Neolithic society and how the monuments were built and used. One room is dedicated to megalithic art and there is also a partial replica of the chamber at Newgrange and one of the sites at Knowth.

NEWGRANGE

This is the best known of the three passage tombs built over 5,000  **Key Sites** years ago – far older than the Egyptian Pyramids. Controversy surrounds the exact usage of Newgrange with many believing that its function was more than a burial tomb. It is exactly positioned so that at dawn on the Winter Solstice a shaft of light penetrates an opening (above the entrance), formed by two

The Entrance Stone at Newgrange.

A view of the monumental mound of Newgrange.

upright slabs of stone topped by a lintel (known as the roof box), and shines down the central passageway lighting up the cross-shaped inner chamber which is usually in complete darkness (see opening photograph).

The mound is about 80 metres (262 ft) in diameter and the passage to the tomb's centre is 20 metres (65 ft) long. The façade of Newgrange has been reconstructed with white quartz stones – many of which were found during excavation. It is estimated that the mound must have taken about 50 years to build and that the stones for the walls and ceilings probably came from a quarry about nine miles away. The quartz may have come from the Wicklow mountains, 50 miles away and granite from the Cooley Mountains, 30 miles away. At the base of the quartz there is a line of huge stone slabs and around the tomb is a stone circle.

The remarkable entrance stone is etched with diamond shapes and double spirals and there are many more such carvings inside. The impressive inner chamber is about 5 metres deep and 6.5 metres wide and huge stones are stacked up to the ceiling with great stones at each corner. Still completely dry and intact, this incredible structure has withstood the weight of over 200,000 tons of soil above it for over five millennia.

Knowth

This mound at the western end of the Brú na Bóinne is encircled by 127 enormous kerbstones and is surrounded by 17 satellite cairns, at least two of which are earlier than the great mound which is slightly larger than Newgrange. 127 is half the 254 sidereal lunar months, which would occur in a 19-year cycle of the Moon.

Inside are two passages aligned to face east and west. The west-facing passage is curved, the other is cruciform, similar to that at Newgrange. Some archaeologists claim that the these passage are aligned with the positions of the rising and setting sun at the spring and autumn equinoxes.

The remains of about 200 people were found within Knowth. In the Stone Age

A PREHISTORIC MOON MAP?

Dr Philip Stooke, a planetary cartographer of the University of Western Ontario in Canada, has stated that an engraving on a stone in the end recess of the passage at Knowth may be the earliest known map of the moon.

' I was amazed when I saw it. Place the markings over a picture of the full Moon and you will see that they line up. It is without doubt a map of the Moon, the most ancient one ever found. It's all there in the carving. You can see the overall pattern of the lunar features such as the Mare Mumorum through to Mare Crisum.' Investigations at Knowth in the 1980s showed that at certain times moonlight could shine down the eastern passage of the tomb which would fall onto the stone.

'The people who carved the Moon map were the first scientists,' said Dr Stooke, 'They knew a great deal about the motion of the Moon. They were not primitive at all.'

bodies were cremated outside and the remains placed in a hollow in special stones within the chamber called basin stones. At Knowth someone attempted to remove the basin stone from the western chamber in about AD 1,000, not appreciating that it was larger than the passage, where it got stuck and remains to this day.

Although visitors cannot go down the passages a special room has been constructed so they can at least see down the eastern passage and appreciate its monumental structure.

The stone carvings at Knowth are numerous – it is estimated that about a quarter of all Europe's known Neolithic art is here. They include what may well be an early sundial and even a map of the Moon (see box above).

DOWTH

Although one can walk around the site of this mound it is not possible to go inside. The mound is surrounded by a kerb of 115 stones, one of which has many sun symbol carvings. The two interior tombs face to the west. The smaller south tomb has a short passage, aligned to the setting sun of the winter solstice, ending in a circular chamber with a recess. Both passage and chamber are illuminated from about 2pm to 4pm on the days around the winter solstice. The north tomb is cross-shaped and contains a large stone basin.

Visitor Information

Opening times

The Visitor Centre is open daily 041 988 0300

March – April 9.30 am – 5.30 pm; May 9.00 am – 6.30 pm; June – Mid-September 9.00 am – 7.00 pm; Mid-End September 9.00 am – 6.30 pm; October 9.30 am – 5.30 pm; November – February 9.30 am – 5.00 pm
041 988 0300 www.brunaboinne@opw.ie www.knowth.com www.heritageireland.ie

How to get there

By car

Via the M1 Motorway;

From the South: Take the M1 north and take the second exit after the toll. This is signed for Donore and Brú na Bóinne. Go through the village of Donore and the Visitor Centre is 2 km (1.5 miles) past the village on the right hand side.

From the North: Take the M1 heading south. Take the first exit after the Boyne Cable Bridge. This is signed for Donore and Brú na Bóinne. Go through the village of Donore and the Visitor Centre is 2 km (1.5 miles) past the village on the right hand side.

From Navan: Take the N51 to Slane. In Slane, turn right towards Dublin on the N2. Take the second turn left. Follow signs for Brú na Bóinne (Newgrange).

From Drogheda: Take the Donore Road from the Bus Station which is located just off the N1 on the south side of the River Boyne. Travel 7 km to the village of Donore, the Visitor Centre is 2 km (1.5 miles) past the village on the right hand side.

From Dublin: Take the N2 north via Ashbourne towards Slane. Turn right about 2 km (1.5 miles) south of Slane. Follow signs for Brú na Bóinne (Newgrange).

From Trim: Take the R161 to Navan. Follow directions from Navan to Slane. In Slane, turn right towards Dublin on the N2. Take the second turn left. Follow signs for Brú na Bóinne (Newgrange).

By bus

Bus Eireann operates a bus service between the Visitor Centre and Drogheda. This service runs in conjunction with the service to Drogheda from Dublin. Contact Bus Eireann, Travel Centre 041 8366111 or 041 983 5023.

Where to Stay

The Glebe House, Dowth 041 983 6101 www.knowth.com/glebehouse

Roughgrange Farmhouse, Donore 041 982 3147 www.irishfarmholidays.com

Gainstown House, Navan 046 21448

Opposite: The extraordinary Giant's Causeway has inspired legends, poets and musicians.

Giant's Causeway and Causeway Coast

A Natural Wonder and a Place of Legend

Date of Inscription 1986

Why is this a World Heritage Site?

The Causeway Coast boasts an unparalleled display of geological formations which represent volcanic activity that took place some 50–60 million years ago during the Tertiary Period. Studies of these formations have made a huge contribution to the development of the earth sciences and knowledge of Tertiary events in the North Atlantic. In addition, the strangeness and beauty of the Giant's Causeway has been a focus for many legends and inspired musicians and poets over the centuries. In 2005 it was voted the fourth greatest natural wonder in the United Kingdom in a popular poll.

Location

The site lies on the north coast of County Antrim, between Causeway Head and Benbane Head, and includes the foreshore, the cliffs, the clifftop path and the car park and visitor facilities at Causeway Head which are run by the National Trust.

DESCRIPTION

The site extends over 70 hectares (175 acres) and is made up of bays and headlands along a 6 km (4 mile) length of coastline. It is the largest remaining lava plateau in the

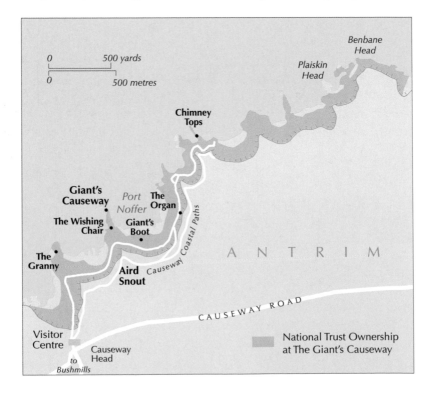

whole of Europe. The Giant's Causeway itself lies at the base of the basalt cliffs and is a dramatic sight. There are about 40,000 huge basalt columns rising out of the sea – they almost look man-made as they are so regular in appearance, many of them hexagonal. The tallest are about 12 metres (40 ft) high and the solidified lava in the cliffs is 28 metres (90 ft) thick in some areas.

'When the world was moulded and fashioned out of formless chaos, this must have been the bit over - a remnant of chaos -' **William Thackeray**

About sixty million years ago the area was the focus of some extraordinary volcanic activity when molten rock was forced through fractures in the chalk bed, thus creating the lava plateau. The basalt lavas, when subjected to rapid cooling, contracted to form the mainly hexagonal columns which we see today.

Other features include the Giant's Organ at Port Noffer consisting of 60 rounded columns each 12 metres (40 ft) high

THE 'DISCOVERY' OF THE CAUSEWAY

In 1693 Sir Richard Bulkeley presented a paper to the Royal Society in which the 'discovery' of remarkable natural phenomena on the Antrim coast was broken to the world at large. Controversy raged as to whether the rock formations had been created by men with chisels, by natural forces or by giants.

Children explore the fascinating shapes of the Basalt columns at the Giant's Causeway.

LEGENDS

Celtic legends relate that the causeway was built by the giant, Finn McCool (Finn mac Cumhaill in Gaelic), so that he could travel from Ireland to Scotland without getting his feet wet. Another place associated with Finn McCool is Fingal's Cave on Staffa – offshore from the Isle of Mull – which like the Giant's Causeway is built up of basaltic columns.

In the 18th century the Scottish poet James Macpherson wrote an epic poem which he claimed was based on ancient texts and written by Finn's son Ossian. The poems gained a wide audience, including Napoleon, and influenced many prominent European writers such as Walter Scott, Goethe, and of course, Mendelssohn who was inspired to write his symphonic poem Fingal's Cave after a visit to Staffa. Schubert also set many of the Ossian poems to music.

resembling huge organ pipes, and the 'Chimney Pots' where a number of columns have come away from the cliffs.

WILDLIFE

This is a haven for birds such as petrels, fulmars, cormorants, shags, redshank, guillemots and razorbills. The rocks also provide a home for many rare plants such as the sea spleenwort, hare's foot trefoil, vernal squill, sea fescue and the frog orchid.

VISITOR INFORMATION

HOW TO GET THERE

BUS SERVICES

Ulsterbus 172, 177. Causeway Coaster minibus from Visitor Centre to stones (NT members free). Causeway Rambler bus (Ulsterbus 376) between Bushmills and Carrick-a-Rede operates in summer. Ulsterbus 252 is a circular route via the Antrim Glens from Belfast. Both stop at the Causeway.

CYCLING

National Cycle Route 93. View local cycle routes on the National Cycle Network website.

BY ROAD

On the B146 Causeway – Dunseverick road 2miles east of Bushmills.

BY TRAIN

Coleraine 10miles or Portrush 8ml. Giant's Causeway & Bushmills Steam Railway, 200yds. 028 2073 2844

ON FOOT

Follow path from Portballintrae alongside steam railway and from Dunservick Castle (4½miles).

NATIONAL TRUST

The site is open daily except for 25 and 26 December. giantscauseway@nationaltrust.org.uk

WHERE TO STAY

The Causeway Hotel, Bushmills 028 2073 1210 www.giants-causeway-hotel.com

Adelphi Hotel, Portrush 028 7082 5544 stay@adelphiportrush.com

Bayview Hotel, Bushmills 028 2073 4100 www.bayviewhotl.com

Skellig Michael

A Remote Place of Pilgrimage in the Wild Atlantic

Date of Inscription 1995

Why is this a World Heritage Site?

The island of Skellig Michael (Michael's Rock) is one of the remotest sacred sites in Europe. The remains of a monastery and a hermitage are spectacularly positioned on the precipitous crags of the island which is set in the Atlantic Ocean. It is an outstanding example of an early Christian monastic settlement deliberately placed in an inaccessible and harsh environment which has led to the preservation and integrity of the monastic structures.

Location

Skellig Michael is about 12 kilometres (7 miles) off the coast of county of Kerry in south west Ireland.

HISTORY

The exact dates of the monastery's foundation are not recorded, however the tradition is that it was founded in the sixth century by St Fionan who was a disciple of St Brendan the Navigator. The first written records come from the end of the eighth century and the dedication of the site to St Michael took place between 950 and 1050.

It was continuously occupied by about 12 monks and their abbot until the 12th century when a period of climate change led to increased storms and gales causing the community to abandon the site. The monks from Skellig Michael became a part of Ballinskelligs Abbey a few miles away on the mainland. In the 16th century Queen Elizabeth I dissolved the Augustinian abbey after the rebellion of the Earl of Desmond who was its protector. The ownership of the island then passed to John Butler but it remained a place of pilgrimage for the devout.

In 1826 John Butler of Waterville sold the island and two lighthouses were built facing the Atlantic. The upper lighthouse was decommissioned in 1870. The ferocity of the forces these lighthouses had to withstand can be gauged by the fact that in December 1955 a wave destroyed the remaining structure even though it was perched 53 metres (175 feet) above the sea. This light was rebuilt in 1967 and was later automated.

In 1880 the island was taken over by the Office of Public Works which still maintains it.

> *'...an incredible, impossible, mad place. I tell you the thing does not belong to any world that you and I have lived and worked in; it is part of our dream world.'*
> **George Bernard Shaw**

There are over 20 island monasteries off the Irish coastline and some near the Hebrides, Orkneys and Shetlands but none as remote as Skellig Michael. Its isolation makes it the earliest, best preserved and most impressive of early Christian monasteries in the Atlantic. (See box on Early Christian Monasticism.)

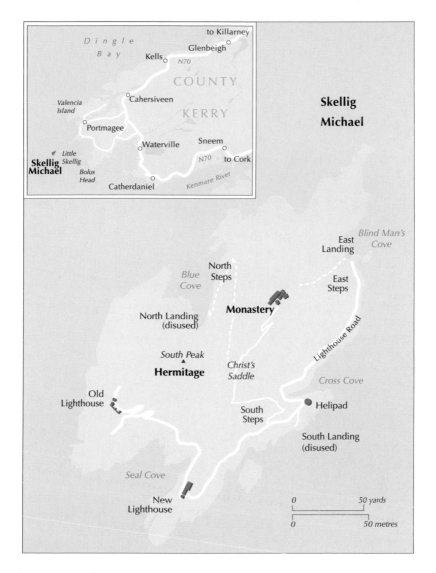

VISITING THE ISLAND

The only route to Skellig Michael is the time-served way of coming by boat. Depending on the state of the sea, landing is possible at three points. From the landing stages there are steep flights of steps to the monastic remains situated on a sloping shelf of the ridge running north-south on the eastern side of the island. The hermitage is on the still steeper South Peak.

The approach to the monastery is via a U-shaped depression in the centre of the island known as as 'Christ's Valley' or 'Christ's saddle' which is flanked by two peaks. There is a narrow strip of terrace over 200 metres (700 ft) above sea level reached by a steep climb of 600 stone steps enclosed by a drystone wall from where a doorway leads to another flight of steps that opens onto a larger enclosure on

A view of the beehive cells with a backdrop of the Irish mainland.

different levels. At the lowest level, facing south and sheltered from the buffeting of the wind, one can see a church, oratories and cells, plus many crosses and cross-slabs. The larger of the oratories are built in coursed stone with an elongated dome. Nearby are the remains of a beehive-shaped toilet cell. St Michael's Church is a rectangular building that would originally have had a timber roof.

The extraordinary beehive-shaped cells when seen from the outside seem to be round but inside they are rectangular and have shelves and sleeping platforms built in to the corbelled stone walls which are almost two metres (six ft) thick. The monks could grow vegetables on the terrace and these, along with bird's eggs and fish, constituted their main diet. There are three freshwater wells on the islet.

VIKING RAIDS

The monks often suffered raids from Viking ships which pillaged the monastery. In the *Annals of Innisfallen* kept by the monks of Innisfallen Abbey near Killarney for the years 433–1450, it was recorded that in 823, 'Skellig was plundered by the heathen and Eitgal (the abbot) was carried off and he died of hunger on their hands.'

Later legends relate that in 993 the Viking Olav Trygvasson, who brought Christianity to Norway and became its king, was baptised by a hermit on Skellig Michael.

THE HERMITAGE

Almost impossible to reach for anyone suffering from vertigo, this group of buildings on the south peak is all but invisible from the lower parts of the rock. Here there are three separate terraces, on one of which the walls of a building still survive.

264

NATURE RESERVE

Skellig Michael and its neighbouring islet, Little Skellig, which appears white from its birdlife and their droppings, are important nature reserves. A vast population of seabirds is attracted here including gannet, fulmar, kittiwake, razorbill, guillemot and puffin. Storm petrels and Manx shearwaters also nest in large numbers.

Common or Bottlenose dolphins, basking sharks, Minke whale and grey seals are all found in the area.

EARLY CHRISTIAN MONASTICISM

'Here on the Skellig, that early eastern tradition of the desert hermit and the ensuing Christian tradition of the monk, merged.' Frank Delaney

The early Christian church always venerated holy men (and sometimes women) who set themselves apart from their fellow human beings and sought a life of stillness the better to worship and contemplate God. The search for solitary asceticism gave us the word for monk from monarchus or 'solitary person'.

In the Middle East this isolation was often to be found in the desert as exemplified by St Antony in the third century. In Ireland these 'deserts' with all the components for an ideal retreat were the small islands in the ocean. The Irish church, untouched by Rome, was an inspirational centre for Christian culture and spirituality and the abbots exercised great influence. The Irish monasteries were also vital centres of learning and the arts.

The remains of the monastery on the edge of the island's precipitous cliffs.

Visitor Information

The nearest large town is Killarney in County Kerry. From the Ring of Kerry road take a junction signposted Renard and Valentia Island Car Ferry. Take the ferry to Knightstown, Valentia Island and follow signs for the fishing village of Portamagee (named after a notorious 18th-century pirate, Theobald Magee). Boats for Skellig (weather permitting) leave from the waterfront of Valentia Island (near to the Skellig Island Experience) and from the pier at Portmagee.

www.skellig,experience.com

Where to Stay

The Moorings Hotel, Portmagee 066 9477108 www.moorings.ie/skelligs

Self-catering cottages, Portmagee 066 9477151 www.portmageeseasidecottages.com

The Ross Hotel, Killarney 064 31855 www.theross.ie

See also www.discoverireland.ie and www.kerrytourist.com

PICTURE CREDITS

The publishers would like to thank the following for the use of their photographs on the following pages:

INDEX